Pingu Learns Hindi

A beginner's guide to Hindi language

Ashutosh Agrawal

About the author and the philosophy behind the book	**10**
Language learning plan	11
Devanagari vs Romanagari	11
Structure of the book	**14**
Chapter 1	**16**
Pingu's introduction	**16**
Your Name & City	17
Hindi is an S-O-V language	19
Maĩ (I)	20
Case 1: Talk about your profession	20
Case 2: Talk about your nationality	21
Case 3: Talk about your faith or preferences	22
Case 4: Talk about your family or relationships	23
Case 5: Talk about your mood	24
Case 6: Talk about your appearance or health	24
Case 7: Miscellaneous cases	25
Postpositions In Hindi	26
Hindi Vocabulary	28
Formula 1	30
Get inspired by HindiUniversity students	31
Chapter 2	**33**
Masculine vs. Feminine	**33**
Gender	34
Rules to determine masculine in Hindi	34
Rule 1: Gender of living things	35
Rule 2: Common nouns ending with "ā"	36
Rule 3: Abstract nouns ending with "nā", "āv", "pun" and "pā"	36
Rule 4: Parts of the body	37
Rule 5: Metals	38
Rule 6: Miscellaneous	38
Rules to determine feminine in Hindi	40
Rule 1: Gender of living things	40
Rule 2: Common nouns ending with the "ī" (ई)	41
Rule 3: Nouns ending with "iya" (िया)	41
Rule 4: Some nouns ending with the "ta" (त) sound	41

Rule 5: Nouns ending with the "kha" (ख) sound	42
Rule 6: Nouns ending with the "at" (अट) sound	42
Rule 7: Miscellaneous	42
Hindi Vocabulary	44
Formula 2	45
Get inspired by HindiUniversity students	46

Chapter 3 — 48

Penguin vs. Penguins In Hindi — 48

Number	49
Plural form of Masculine Nouns	49
Marked Nouns	49
Unmarked Nouns	50
Plural form of Feminine Nouns	51
Marked Nouns	51
Unmarked Nouns	52
Kā/Kī and Ke (का/की and के)	54
Using "Kā" (का) in Hindi	54
Using "Ke" (के) in Hindi	55
Using "Kī" (की) in Hindi	56
Formula 3	58
Get inspired by HindiUniversity students	59

Chapter 4 — 61

Hindi Pronouns — 61

Personal Pronouns (I, You, We, They, he, she, it)	62
Demonstrative Pronouns	65
Possessive Pronouns	67
Hindi Vocabulary	69
Get inspired by HindiUniversity students	70

Chapter 5 — 72

Pingu's daily routine — 72

Present Indefinite Tense	73
Hindi Verbs	73
Present Indefinite Tense - Affirmative Sentences	75
Present Indefinite Tense - Negative Sentence	78
Case 1: Using the negative form when there is no action verb	78
Case 2: Using the negative form when there is an action verb.	79

Present Indefinite Tense - Interrogative Sentence	80
Case 1: Using the interrogative form when there is no action verb	80
Case 2: Using the interrogative form, when there is an action verb.	81
Present Indefinite Tense - Interrogative Negative Sentence	82
Case 1: Using the interrogative-negative form, when there is no action verb	82
Case 2: Using the negative interrogative form when there is an action verb.	83
Get inspired by HindiUniversity students	84

Chapter 6 — 86

What is Pingu doing right now? — 86

Present Continuous Tense	87
Hindi Vocabulary	91
Get inspired by HindiUniversity students	92

Chapter 7 — 94

Pingu's future plans — 94

Future Indefinite Tense	95
Hindi Vocabulary	99
Get inspired by HindiUniversity students	100

Chapter 8 — 102

Things Pingu used to do — 102

Past Indefinite	103
Case 1: Using the past forms of "to be"	104
Case 2: Using the "action verbs"	104
Hindi Vocabulary	108
Get inspired by HindiUniversity students	109

Chapter 9 — 111

What did Pingu do? — 111

Past Tense	111
Transitive vs. Intransitive Verbs	112
Transitive Verbs	112
Intransitive Verbs	112
Using intransitive verbs in the past tense	115
Using transitive verbs in the past tense	118
Hindi Vocabulary	122
Get inspired by HindiUniversity students	123

Chapter 10 — 125

What can Pingu do? **125**
    Modal Verbs 125
        Modal Verb: Can 126
        Modal Verb: Could 129
        Modal Verb: May 131
        Modal Verb: To want 132
        Modal Verb: Should 132
        Scenario 1: Doctor's advice to a patient 134
        Scenario 2: Giving advice 135
    Hindi Vocabulary 136
    Gt inspired by HindiUniversity students 137

Chapter 11 .... **139**

Pingu is sitting on an iceberg **139**
    Hindi Postpositions 140
        Postpostion: Pe/Par पे/पर (On) 140
        Postpostion: Ke liye के लिए (For) 141
    Postpostion: Ko को (to) 143
        Type 1: If you need something 144
        Type 2: If you like someone or something 145
        Type 3: If you have a particular symptom 146
        Type 4: You have information about something 147
        Type 5: To describe abstract nouns 148
    Postpositions after nouns 150
        Rule 1: Postposition after masculine singular nouns: 151
        Rule 2: Postposition after masculine plural nouns: 151
        Rule 3: Postposition after feminine singular nouns: 152
        Rule 4: Postposition after feminine plural nouns: 153
    Post positions after pronouns 155
    Hindi Vocabulary 157
        Conversation Between Kevin and Maddy 158
    Get inspired by HindiUniversity students 159

Chapter 12 .... **161**

Pingu asks questions **161**
    Hindi Interrogatives 162
        What - Kyā क्या 162
            Case 1 163
            Case 2 163

Where - Kahā̃ कहाँ	166
Case 1	166
Case 2	167
How - Kaisā कैसा / Kaisī कैसी / Kaise कैसे	168
When - Kab कब	170
Who - Kaun कौन	170
Which - Kaun sā कौन सा / Kaun se कौन से / Kaun sī कौन सी	172
Why - Kyō̃ क्यों	173
Hindi Vocabulary	175
Conversation Between Mara and Nora	176
Conversation Between Ady and Nora	177

Chapter 13 — 179

Pingu is beautiful — 179

Adjectives	179
Case 1: Inflected adjectives	180
Case 2: Uninflected adjectives	182
Case 3: Using post-positions with adjectives	183
Case 4: Making advanced sentences using adjectives	185
Hindi Vocabulary	187
Get inspired by HindiUniversity students	189

Chapter 14 — 189

Pingu was walking slowly — 191

Adverbs	191
Adverbs that answer "How"	192
Adverbs that answer "When"	194
Adverbs that answer "Where"	195
Adverbs that answer "To what extent"	196
Language learning Patterns	198
Get inspired by HindiUniversity students	199

Answer Sheet — 200

CHAPTER 1	200
Exercise 1.1	200
Exercise 1.2	200
Exercise 1.3	200
Exercise 1.4	200
Exercise 1.5	200
Exercise 1.6	200

Exercise 1.7	201
Exercise 1.8	201
Exercise 1.9	201
Exercise 1.10	201
Exercise 1.11	201
CHAPTER 2	**202**
Exercise 2.1	202
CHAPTER 3	**202**
Exercise 3.1	202
Exercise 3.2	202
Exercise 3.3	202
Exercise 3.4	203
Exercise 3.5	203
Exercise 3.6	203
Exercise 3.7	203
Exercise 3.8	203
CHAPTER 4	**204**
Exercise 4.1	204
Exercise 4.2	204
Exercise 4.3	204
Exercise 4.4	205
Exercise 4.5	205
Exercise 4.6	205
Exercise 4.7	205
CHAPTER 5	**206**
Exercise 5.1	206
Exercise 5.2	206
Exercise 5.3	206
Exercise 5.4	207
Exercise 5.5	207
Exercise 5.6	207
Exercise 5.7	207
Exercise 5.8	208
CHAPTER 6	**208**
Exercise 6.1	208
Exercise 6.2	209
Exercise 6.3	209
Exercise 6.4	209
CHAPTER 7	**210**

Exercise 7.1	210
Exercise 7.2	210
Exercise 7.3	211
Exercise 7.4	211
Exercise 7.5	211
CHAPTER 8	212
Exercise 8.1	212
Exercise 8.2	212
Exercise 8.3	212
Exercise 8.4	213
Exercise 8.5	213
CHAPTER 9	214
Exercise 9.1	214
Exercise 9.2	214
Exercise 9.3	214
Exercise 9.4	215
Exercise 9.5	215
Exercise 9.6	215
Exercise 9.7	216
Exercise 9.8	216
Exercise 9.9	216
CHAPTER 10	217
Exercise 10.1	217
Exercise 10.2	217
Exercise 10.3	218
CHAPTER 11	219
Exercise 11.1	219
Exercise 11.2	219
Exercise 11.3	219
Exercise 11.4	220
Exercise 11.5	221
Exercise 11.6	221
Exercise 11.7	221
Exercise 11.8	221
Exercise 11.9	222
Exercise 11.10	222
Exercise 11.11	223
CHAPTER 12	223
Exercise 12.1	223

Exercise 12.2	223
Exercise 12.3	224
Exercise 12.4	224
Exercise 12.5	224
Exercise 12.6	224
Exercise 12.7	225
CHAPTER 13	225
Exercise 13.1	225
Exercise 13.2	225
Exercise 13.3	226
CHAPTER 14	226
Exercise 14.1	226
Exercise 14.2	227
Exercise 14.3	227
Exercise 14.4	227
Exercise 14.5	228
What's next?	**228**
To the reader	**231**

Hello and Welcome to HindiUniversity! This book is written by Ashu ji and his students at *HindiUniversity*. The group consists of students from 100+ countries - every continent, except Antarctica.

We have met a little penguin from Antarctica who wants to learn Hindi and about Indian culture. Her name is Pingu. She likes Bollywood movies, cricket, and swimming. Come join us on Pingu's journey to speaking Hindi!

About the author and the philosophy behind the book

Namaste,

My name is Ashutosh. I live in San Francisco, USA. I am a teacher by hobby and a software engineer by profession. The HindiUniversity project began in 2008 with the simple desire to contribute to my community.

I started out with teaching Hindi for the Global Language Network (GLN) at George Washington University, as a fun after-work activity. While teaching there, I realized that I could reach thousands of interested students using an online forum. With this seed of an idea, I set up *HindiUniversity* on YouTube with just a small whiteboard and a simple camera. To my surprise, the response to the videos was incredible. As it turned out, Hindi enthusiasts across the globe had been waiting for something like this to come along, which immersed them in Hindi from the very beginning, without requiring knowledge of the script or the alphabet. That is how the project got started,
http://www.youtube.com/hindiuniversity

The HindiUniversity project is solely dependent on social media for reaching global learners. My courses are available on Youtube, Facebook, and Twitter. I am really excited that you are joining me in this journey. I am confident that the book will provide you with a solid foundation to speak the Hindi language. You will have the confidence to ask questions in Hindi and won't feel uncomfortable speaking to native Hindi speakers.

Language learning plan

As you go through the book, I want you to build a Hindi language learning plan. There are five essential aspects of a language learning plan:

- Find a language buddy, someone you can practice with, without being afraid of making mistakes. Find someone who is genuinely interested in seeing you grow and keeps your morale high throughout the process.
- Set a timeline: Set a target date to complete the book and start using it in a daily Hindi conversation. I believe two months are more than enough to read the book a few times, complete all the exercises, and start practicing.
- Follow the process: I have written all the chapters in a particular sequence and highly recommend you stick to maximize the language learning experience. It is very easy to get distracted and jump from one topic to another, one video to another, and so on.
- Keep a journal: I highly recommend you maintain a small journal where you can track and measure your progress on a regular basis. Write down new sentences as you learn and use them. If you make any mistakes, please write them down in the journal. Try the same sentences again and again till you master them.
- Practice, Practice, Practice: There is no other way to learn a new language. I will provide a lot of useful tips and tools throughout the book. To practice more formally, you can join me live every Sunday for free Hindi lessons. You can also follow the HindiUniversity YouTube channel. (YouTube.com/HindiUniversity)

Devanagari vs Romanagari

I have come across this question several times in the past 14 years. Why don't you write all the sentences in the Devanagari script. While it's important that you learn Devanagari script, this book will focus on common patterns in the Hindi language.

My goal is to make sure you feel comfortable in Hindi conversation. When a child learns to speak any language, their focus for the first 3 to 4 years is simply to mimic what everyone is saying and responding in the same manner. I believe once you can speak confidently, learning Devanagari would be more fun afterward.

This book is developed for a beginner level with no prerequisite of knowing the Devanagari script. After completing each chapter, I highly encourage you to watch my videos referenced throughout the book to learn the correct pronunciations. In general, I find it more useful to discuss the proper pronunciation during the live interaction/class than debating the Hindi transliteration.

This is not an academic book to help you receive any college credits, or master the comprehensive Hindi grammar. Rather, the focus is to teach you minimal Hindi grammar to get the conversation going. The right audience for this book is someone going to India for the first time and wanting to interact with locals in Hindi, someone who enjoys speaking multiple languages, or someone wanting to learn conversational Hindi quickly and confidently using simple grammar rules and patterns.

You will find some special symbols throughout the book to help you distinguish between short, long, and nasalized vowels. Below, you can find some examples for the short and long vowels so you can familiarize yourself with these sounds.

Vowel			Hindi Examples		English Examples	
a	अ	Short *a*	akhbār	अख़बार	but	/bʌt/
ā	आ	Long *a*	ādmī	आदमी	father	/ˈfɑːðə/
i	इ	Short *i*	imārat	इमारत	sit	/sɪt/
ī	ई	Long *i*	īmāndār	ईमानदार	need	/niːd/
u	उ	Short *u*	uttar	उत्तर	book	/bʊk/
ū	ऊ	Long *u*	ūn	ऊन	soon	/suːn/
e	ए	Short *e*	ek	एक	mane	/meɪn/
ai	ऐ	Long *e*	ainak	ऐनक	hay	/heɪ/
o	ओ	Short *o*	olā	ओला	both	/bəʊθ/
au	औ	Long *o*	aurat	औरत	saw	/sɔː/

All the nasalized vowels, either short or long, are represented by a small wave on top of the letter. In the case of the sounds "ai" and "au", the wave goes on top of the "ı" and "u": aĩ & aũ

Short	Hindi word		Long	Hindi word	
ã	Hãsnā	हँसना	ā̃	ghariyā̃	घड़ियाँ
ĩ	sĩncāī	सिंचाई	ī̃	nahī̃	नहीं
ũ	mũch	मुँह	ū̃	ū̃t	ऊँट
ẽ	kitābẽ	किताबें	aĩ	maĩ	मैं
õ	kyõ	क्यों	aũ	bhaũ	भौं

Structure of the book

The book has 14 chapters. The chapters are organized in a particular intended sequence. In my teaching experience, and while conducting HindiUniversity classes, I have realized that this order makes a big difference. My goal is to make sure there is an outcome for each chapter.

Chapter	Goal & Outcome
1	To be able to introduce yourself In Hindi and form basic sentences.
2	To be able to differentiate between Hindi masculine and feminine nouns.
3	To learn and master Hindi singular and plurals.
4	To learn about Hindi pronouns and use them in simple conversations.
5	To talk about your daily routine in Hindi.
6	To talk about things you are currently doing.
7	To talk about your future plans in Hindi.
8	To feel comfortable talking about things you used to do in the past.
9	To talk about the mistakes you made, the food you ate, and the movies you watched in Hindi.
10	To express your abilities, possibility of something happening, to seek permission in Hindi.
11	To learn about important post-positions in Hindi and be able to say what you need, what you can do for others, and where you are in Hindi.
12	To be able to ask questions in Hindi.
13	To be able to start making advanced sentences using Hindi Adjectives.
14	To be able to start making advanced sentences using Hindi Adverbs.

Once again, congratulations .. and happy learning. I am really proud of you.

Ashutosh A

Chapter 1
Pingu's introduction

- Pingu is determined to learn Hindi. By the end of this chapter, she will introduce herself in Hindi (with minimal grammar).

In this chapter, Pingu (our little penguin) will learn to introduce herself in Hindi. She will also learn the Hindi pronoun (Maĩ), Hindi post-positions (Se, Mẽ), and construct simple Hindi sentences. Pingu is not alone in this journey. She is joined by several passionate Hindi learners who will happily teach her. Let's meet some of them:

Your Name & City

- My name is Saida. I am from Morocco.

- Merā nām Saida hai. Maĩ Morocco *se* hũ.
- मेरा नाम Saida है । मैं Morocco से हूँ ।

- My name is Simon. I am from Sweden.

- Merā nām Simon hai. Maĩ Sweden *se* hũ.
- मेरा नाम Simon है । मैं Sweden से हूँ ।

- My name is Ifigenia. I am from Greece.

- Merā nām Ifigenia hai. Maĩ Greece *se* hũ.
- मेरा नाम Ifigenia है । मैं Greece से हूँ ।

- My name is Adam, and I am from the USA.

- Merā nām Adam hai aur maĩ USA *se* hũ.
- मेरा नाम Adam है और मैं USA से हूँ ।

Now, let's try to read the following sentences but without any English translation.

- Namaste, merā nām Alejandra hai aur maĩ Colombia *se* hũ.
- नमस्ते, मेरा नाम Alejandra है और मैं Colombia से हूँ ।

- Merā nām Aisha hai aur maĩ Norway *se* hũ.
- मेरा नाम Aisha है और मैं Norway से हूँ ।

- Merā nām Edith hai aur maĩ Mexico *se* hũ.
- मेरा नाम Edith है और मैं Mexico से हूँ ।

- Merā nām Andrea hai. Maĩ Germany *se* hū̃.
- मेरा नाम Andrea है । मैं Germany से हूँ ।

- Namaskār dostō. Merā nām Stefan hai aur maĩ Serbia *se* hū̃.
- नमस्कार दोस्तों । मेरा नाम Stefan है और मैं Serbia से हूँ ।

You will notice a common pattern in all of the above Hindi sentences. First, the students tell their <u>name,</u> then the place they are <u>from</u>.

- Merā nām __(insert name)__ hai.
- My name is _____ .

- Maĩ __(insert country)__ se hū̃.
- I am from _____ .

Do you want to practice introducing yourself in Hindi with Pingu? Go ahead and help her complete the challenge.

Exercise 1.1 Introduce your name and place of origin in Hindi.

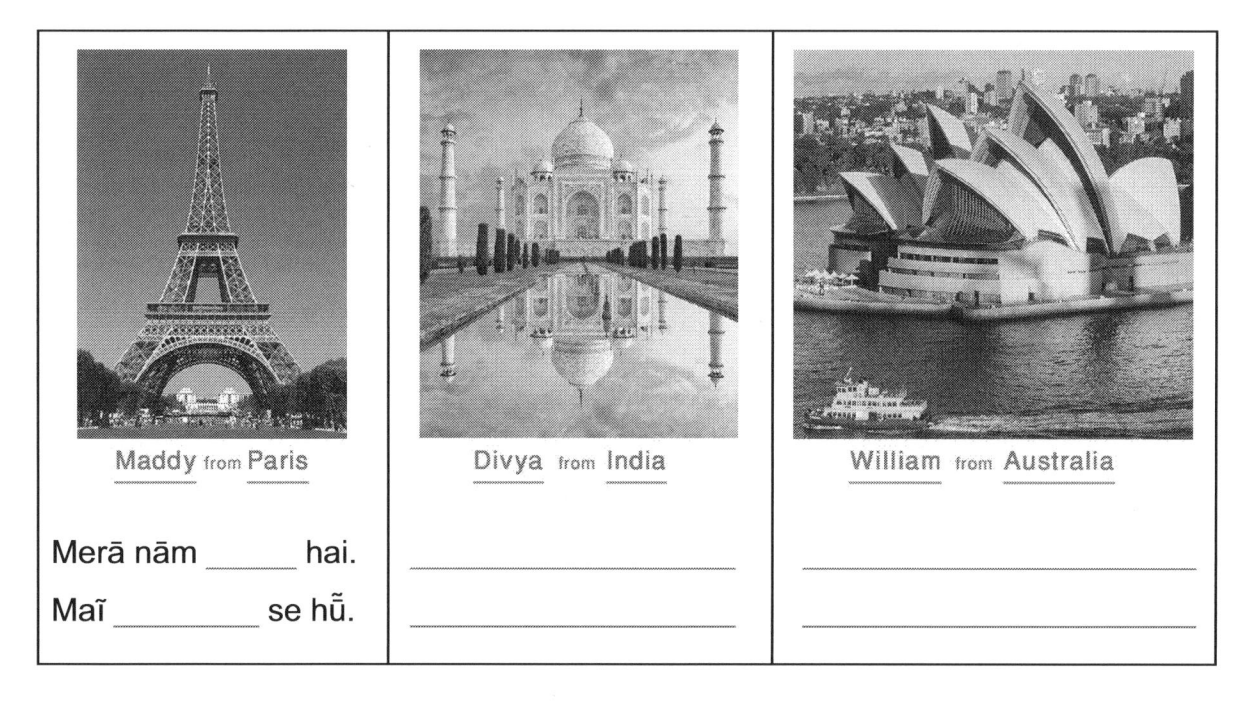

Maddy from Paris	Divya from India	William from Australia
Merā nām _____ hai. Maĩ _____ se hū̃.	_____ _____	_____ _____

<u>Observation 1</u>: Did you notice any new Hindi words so far? Write them down and we will revisit them later in the book.

Hindi is an S-O-V language

Hindi is considered an S-O-V language. In a typical sentence, you will write the "Subject" followed by an "Object" followed by a "Verb". However, English is an S-V-O language. Let's see an example in English first.

I	learn	Hindi
(*Subject*)	(*Verb*)	(*Object*)

I	love	him
(*Subject*)	(*Verb*)	(*Object*)

Now, let's see the same sentence in Hindi. You will notice the S-0-V pattern. SOV here stands for Subject-Object-Verb.

Maĩ	Hindī	sīkhtā hū̃.
मैं	हिन्दी	सीखता हूँ ।
(*Subject*)	(*Object*)	(*Verb*)

Observation 2: I am curious to know what patterns are used in your native language. Share your observation below.

My native language is: _____
My native language follows this pattern: _____

The S-O-V order is used by the largest number of distinct languages in the world. This also includes Hindi, other languages from the Indian subcontinent, and the Dravidian languages (spoken primarily in southern India and parts of eastern and central India). As per Wikipedia, 45% of the world's languages use the S-O-V order [source].

Maĩ (I)

"Maĩ" मैं is a personal pronoun in Hindi, which means "I". As you start to learn Hindi, you will be using this pronoun frequently.

In Hindi "am" is "hũ" हूँ. It's pronounced as "hoo" with a nasalized vowel "n". Following is a simple construction for a sentence that uses "Maĩ" and "hũ" together:

- I am _____ .
- Maĩ _____ hũ.
- मैं _____ हूँ |

In Cases 1 to 7 below, we will cover seven scenarios on how you can use this construction (Maĩ _____ hũ) to form a variety of Hindi sentences to introduce or express yourself. Some examples are provided below:

- I am Pingu.
- I am a global citizen.
- I am a bird.
- I am a swimmer.
- I am excited.
- I am thankful.

Case 1: Talk about your profession

- I am an engineer.
  - Maĩ engineer hũ.
  - मैं engineer हूँ |

- I am a traveler.
  - Maĩ traveler hũ.
  - मैं traveller हूँ |

- I am a student.
  - Maĩ student hũ.
  - मैं student हूँ |

- I am a teacher.
  - Maĩ teacher hũ.
  - मैं teacher हूँ |

- I am a businessman.
- I am a farmer.

- Maĩ businessman hũ.
- मैं businessman हूँ।

- Maĩ farmer hũ.
- मैं farmer हूँ।

Exercise 1.2 Write your profession in Hindi.

Maĩ _____ hũ.

Case 2: Talk about your nationality

- I am an Indian.
  - Maĩ Indian hũ.
  - मैं Indian हूँ।

- I am an American.
  - Maĩ American hũ.
  - मैं American हूँ।

- I am Spanish.
  - Maĩ Spanish hũ.
  - मैं Spanish हूँ।

- I am French.
  - Maĩ French hũ.
  - मैं French हूँ।

- I am Chinese.
  - Maĩ Chinese hũ.
  - मैं Chinese हूँ।

Exercise 1.3 Write your nationality in Hindi.

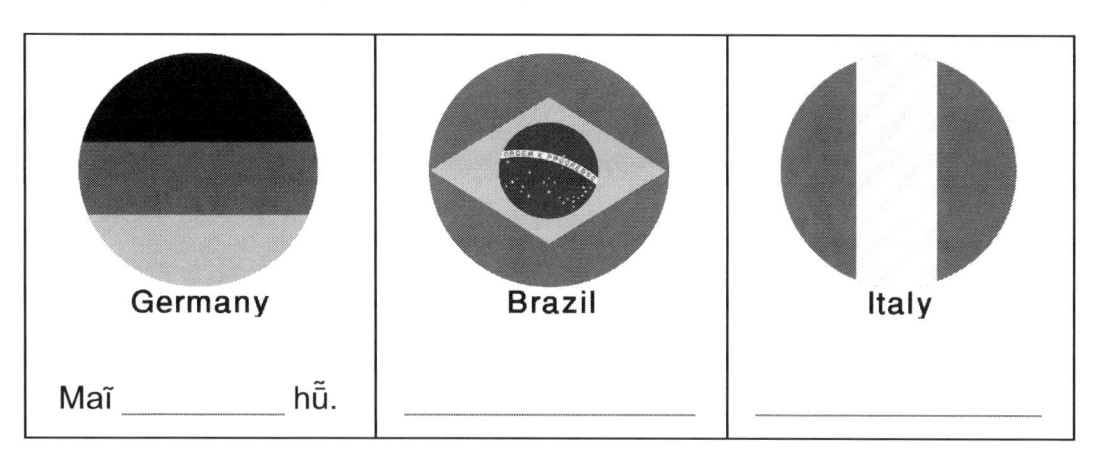

Germany	Brazil	Italy
Maĩ _____ hũ.	_____	_____

Case 3: Talk about your faith or preferences

- I am a vegetarian.
- Maĩ vegetarian hũ.
- मैं vegetarian हूँ ।

- I am a vegan.
- Maĩ vegan hũ.
- मैं vegan हूँ ।

- I am a Buddhist.
- Maĩ Buddhist hũ.
- मैं Buddhist हूँ ।

- I am a conservative.
- Maĩ conservative hũ.
- मैं conservative हूँ ।

- I am a yogi.
- Maĩ yogi hũ.
- मैं yogi हूँ ।

- I am a socialist
- Maĩ socialist hũ.
- मैं socialist हूँ ।

Exercise 1.4 Help Pingu construct sentences using the given words.

| philosopher | coin collector | diabetic | Christian |

1 _____
2 _____
3 _____
4 _____

Case 4: Talk about your family or relationships

- I am a mother.
  - Maĩ mã̄ hū̃.
  - मैं माँ हूँ ।

- I am a father.
  - Maĩ pitā hū̃.
  - मैं पिता हूँ ।

- I am a relative.
  - Maĩ relative hū̃.
  - मैं relative हूँ ।

- I am a child.
  - Maĩ baccā hū̃.
  - मैं बच्चा हूँ ।

- I am single.
  - Maĩ single hū̃.
  - मैं single हूँ ।

- I am married.
  - Maĩ married hū̃.
  - मैं married हूँ ।

Exercise 1.5 Help Pingu form Hindi sentences on the visuals below.

Maĩ _____ hū̃.

Case 5: Talk about your mood

- I am upset.
- I am happy.
- I am worried.
- I am satisfied.
- I am restless.

- Maĩ nārāz hũ.
- मैं नाराज़ हूँ ।
- Maĩ khush hũ.
- मैं खुश हूँ ।
- Maĩ pareshān hũ.
- मैं परेशान हूँ ।
- Maĩ satisfied hũ.
- मैं satisfied हूँ ।
- Maĩ bechain hũ.
- मैं बेचैन हूँ ।

Exercise 1.6 Help pingu make "I am" sentences using the words in the table.

| nervous | calm | angry | excited |

1 _____
2 _____
3 _____
4 _____

Case 6: Talk about your appearance or health

- I am tall.
- I am healthy.
- I am sick.
- I am alright.

- Maĩ tall hũ.
- मैं tall हूँ ।
- Maĩ healthy hũ.
- मैं healthy हूँ ।
- Maĩ bīmār hũ.
- मैं बीमार हूँ ।
- Maĩ thīk hũ.
- मैं ठीक हूँ ।

Exercise 1.7 Can you help Pingu think of a similar example?

Maĩ _____ hũ.

Case 7: Miscellaneous cases

- I am right.
- I am wrong.
- I am a stranger.
- I am middle class.
- I am loyal.
- I am a cricket fan.

- Maĩ sahī hũ.
- मैं सही हूँ ।

- Maĩ galat hũ.
- मैं गलत हूँ ।

- Maĩ stranger hũ.
- मैं stranger हूँ ।

- Maĩ middle class hũ.
- मैं middle class हूँ ।

- Maĩ sacchā hũ.
- मैं सच्चा हूँ ।

- Maĩ cricket fan hũ.
- मैं cricket fan हूँ ।

Exercise 1.8 Can you help Pingu form similar Hindi sentences?

Watch the video "Introduction in HIndi" at YouTube.com/HindiUniversity (playlist: Pingu Learns To Speak Hindi) to deepen your learning.

Postpositions In Hindi

The next step is to learn some key postpositions in Hindi. The concept of postpositions in Hindi is exactly the same as prepositions in English. In Hindi, these keywords come after the nouns, which is why they are known as postpositions instead of prepositions.

In this section, we will learn two postpositions:

- Se (से)   - from
- Mẽ (में) - in

Let's see how these postpositions are used:

- From Paris   =   Paris se
- From Delhi   =   Delhi se
- From School =   School se
- From where   =   Kahã se

Now let's use them in sentences.

- I am from Paris.
- Maĩ Paris se hũ.
- मैं Paris से हूँ ।

- I am from the UK.
- Maĩ UK se hũ.
- मैं UK से हूँ ।

Exercise 1.9 Help Pingu translate the following sentences in Hindi.

1. I am from India: _____ .
2. I am from Taiwan: _____ .

Similarly, let's use "Mẽ" in simple sentences.

- in the train   - train mẽ
- in the elevator - elevator mẽ
- in the class   - class mẽ
- in Delhi   - Delhi mẽ

That was easy; let's make full sentences now:

- I am in the elevator.
- I am in Sydney.
- I am in the class.
- I am in the zoo.

- Maĩ elevator mẽ hũ.
- मैं elevator में हूँ ।
- Maĩ Sydney mẽ hũ.
- मैं Sydney में हूँ ।
- Maĩ class mẽ hũ.
- मैं class में हूँ ।
- Maĩ zoo mẽ hũ.
- मैं zoo में हूँ ।

Now if someone is asking you where you are from, you will be able to answer them in Hindi. Complete the following challenge to check your understanding.

Exercise 1.10 Translate the following sentences in Hindi.

1 I am in Nepal: _____ .

2 I am in School: _____ .

> Watch the videos "Hindi Postposition - 1" & "Hindi Postposition - 2" at YouTube.com/HindiUniversity to deepen your learning.

---

if you can learn the basic building blocks of a foreign language and learn to repeat them effectively, learning a new language can be fun. The American designer Dan Phillips has said:

"It doesn't matter if you don't have a complete set of anything because repetition creates pattern, repetition creates pattern, repetition creates pattern"

Hindi Vocabulary

In this chapter, you have learned how to introduce yourself in simple Hindi sentences. Now, I want you to build some vocabulary in Hindi. The idea is to use these words often, so they become part of your regular Hindi conversation.

English	Hindi	Devanagari
Brother	Bhāī	भाई
Buddhist	Bauddh	बौद्ध
Businessman	Vyavasāyī	व्यवसायी
Conservative	Aparivartanavādī	अपरिवर्तनवादी
Cricket fan	Kriket Prashāsak	क्रिकेट प्रशंसक
Daughter	Betī	बेटी
Engineer	Ĩjīniyar	इंजीनियर
Farmer	Kisān	किसान
Father	Pitā	पिता
Happy	Khush	खुश
Healthy	Svasth	स्वस्थ
Hello	Namaste	नमस्ते
Indian	Bhārtīya	भारतीय
Loyal	Sacchā	सच्चा
Married	Vivāhit	विवाहित
Middle class	Madhyam Vargīy	मध्यम वर्गीय
Mother	Mã̄	माँ
Name	Nām	नाम

Nature lover	Prakriti Premī	प्रकृति प्रेमी
Relative	Rishtedār	रिश्तेदार
Restless	Bechain	बेचैन
Right	Sahī	सही
Satisfied	Santusht	संतुष्ट
Short (*male*)	Chhotā	छोटा
Short (*female*)	Chhotī	छोटी
Sick	Bīmār	बीमार
Single	Akelā	अकेला
Son	Betā	बेटा
Stranger	Ajnabī	अजनबी
Student (*male*)	Chhātr	छात्र
Student (*female*)	Chhātrā	छात्रा
Tall (*male*)	Lambā	लंबा
Tall (*female*)	Lambī	लंबी
Teacher	Adhyāpak	अध्यापक
Thin (*male*)	Patlā	पतला
Thin (*female*)	Patlī	पतली
Traveller	Yātrī	यात्री
Upset	Nārāz	नाराज़
Vegetarian	Shākāhārī	शाकाहारी
Worried	Pareshān	परेशान
Wrong	Galat	गलत

Formula 1

As you start learning Hindi, you will find it hard to recall many Hindi words. The good news is that you don't need to memorize hundreds of words when you are just starting out. A common question students often ask me is *"How do you say this in Hindi"*? Here, I will teach you how to ask this same question in Hindi.

Here we go:

- How do you say _____ in Hindi?   (English)
- Hindī mẽ _____ ko kyā kehte haĩ?   (Romanagari)
- हिन्दी में _____ को क्या कहते हैं ?   (Devanagari)

Imagine that you do not know the Hindi word for "Tree" or "River". You can still construct a simple Hindi sentence using the formula below:

- Hindī mẽ Tree ko kyā kehte haĩ?
- Hindī mẽ River ko kyā kehte haĩ?

The person you are speaking with will gladly tell you the answer and you will get practice saying the formula in a conversation:

- Hindī mẽ Tree ko Ped kehte haĩ. (Tree is called 'Ped' in Hindi)
- Hindī mẽ River ko Nadī kehte haĩ. (River is called 'Nadī' in Hindi)

Here you have turned your need into an opportunity to practice conversation in Hindi. You can use this technique and find out what a particular word is called in Hindi. You will also be able to impress your friends as you ask questions in Hindi.

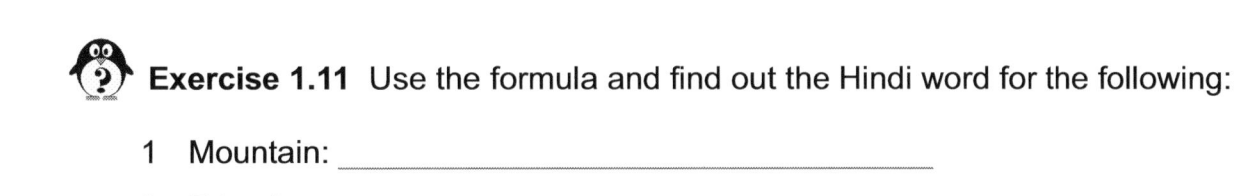

Exercise 1.11 Use the formula and find out the Hindi word for the following:

1 Mountain: _____
2 Friend: _____

Get inspired by HindiUniversity students

After going through similar sessions, my students wrote essays to introduce themselves in Hindi. If you go through them, not only will you refresh your concepts, but will also pick up some new words and sentences.

Lizett

Maĩ Lizett hũ aur maĩ Bolivia se hũ.

मैं Lizett हूँ और मैं Bolivia से हूँ ।

Lorena

Merā nām Lorena hai, maĩ Stockholm mẽ rehtī hũ.

मेरा नाम Lorena है । मैं Stockholm में रहती हूँ ।

Sarah

Merā nām Sarah hai. Maĩ Sacramento, CA mẽ rehtī hũ. Maĩ 2014 se Hindī padh rahī hũ.

मेरा नाम Sarah है । मैं Sacramento, CA में रहती हूँ । मैं 2014 से हिन्दी पढ़ रही हूँ ।

Mayte

Merā nām Mayte hai. Maĩ Spain se hũ aur do sāl se Hindī sīkh rahī hũ. Āpse milkar bahut khushī huī.

मेरा नाम Mayte है । मैं Spain से हूँ और दो साल से हिन्दी सीख रही हूँ । आपसे मिलकर बहुत ख़ुशी हुई ।

As promised, let's make sure Pingu can introduce herself in Hindi.

Pingu

Namaste! Merā nām Pingu hai. Maĩ Antarctica se hũ. Maĩ bird (chidiyā) hũ!

नमस्ते ! मेरा नाम Pingu है । मैं Antarctica से हूँ । मैं चिड़िया हूँ ।

Chapter 2

Masculine vs. Feminine

† In this chapter, Pingu will be able to differentiate between Hindi masculine and feminine and will have the tools to ask questions and clarify if a particular noun is masculine or feminine.

Gender

Pingu is now familiar with a personal pronoun, Maĩ (I), and two postpositions, Se (from) and Mẽ (in). However, she is curious about gender in Hindi.

In Chapter 2, she will learn about gender in Hindi. It's essential to know a word's gender to decline the noun (i.e., use a correct form) and to modify other words related to the noun within a sentence.

In English, you will say "Pingu's school" or "Pingu's bag" to show that it's her school or bag. You do not need to know the gender of the *bag* or the *school*. However, In Hindi, you will need to know the gender of *bag* and *school* to show the relationship between "Pingu" and the "things possessed" by Pingu. You will learn about it later in this chapter and the next chapter.

Every living and non-living object in Hindi can be classified into a particular gender: *Masculine* or *Feminine*. Even material objects like table, chair, car have gender in Hindi. This topic can be confusing for new Hindi learners as there is no easy way to determine if the noun is masculine or feminine. We will learn basic rules to make it a bit easier.

Rules to determine masculine in Hindi

The rules will help you identify the differences between masculine and feminine nouns.

I will also provide formulae to determine the gender for animals, and other non-living things like metals, gases, chairs, pizza, etc.

Rule 1: Gender of living things

This rule is straightforward and works exactly like other languages. Nouns referring to males such as boy, dad, and uncle are considered "masculine".

English Nouns (masculine)	Hindi Nouns (masculine)	Devanagari
Boy	Ladkā	लड़का
Brother	Bhāī	भाई
Brother-in-law	Jījā	जीजा
Child	Bacchā	बच्चा
Father	Pitā	पिता
Grandfather (maternal)	Nānā	नाना
Grandfather (paternal)	Dādā	दादा
Nephew (brother's son)	Bhatījā	भतीजा
Nephew (sister's son)	Bhā̃jā	भाँजा
Uncle (maternal)	Māmā	मामा
Uncle (paternal)	Chāchā	चाचा
Male Horse	Ghodā	घोड़ा
Male Dog	Kuttā	कुत्ता
Male Donkey	Gadhā	गधा

Rule 2: Common nouns ending with "ā"

Common nouns (non-specific person, place or thing) ending with "ā" are often considered "masculine" in Hindi. Let's not worry about the exceptions to this rule just yet.

- Cloth = Kapdā   कपड़ा
- Money = Paisā   पैसा
- Room = Kamrā   कमरा

Rule 3: Abstract nouns ending with "nā", "āv", "pun" and "pā"

Abstract nouns ending with "nā", "āv", "pun" and "pā" are considered masculine in Hindi. Examples include the following:

Ending with nā (ना)

- Song = Gānā   गाना
- Food = Khānā   खाना

Ending with āv (आव)

- Attachment = Lagāv   लगाव
- Flow = Bahāv   बहाव

Ending with pun (पन)

- Childhood = Bachpun   बचपन
- Boyhood = Ladakpun   लड़कपन
- Madness = Pāgalpun   पागलपन

Ending with pā (पा)

- Obesity = Motāpā   मोटापा
- Old age = Budhāpā   बुढ़ापा

Rule 4: Parts of the body

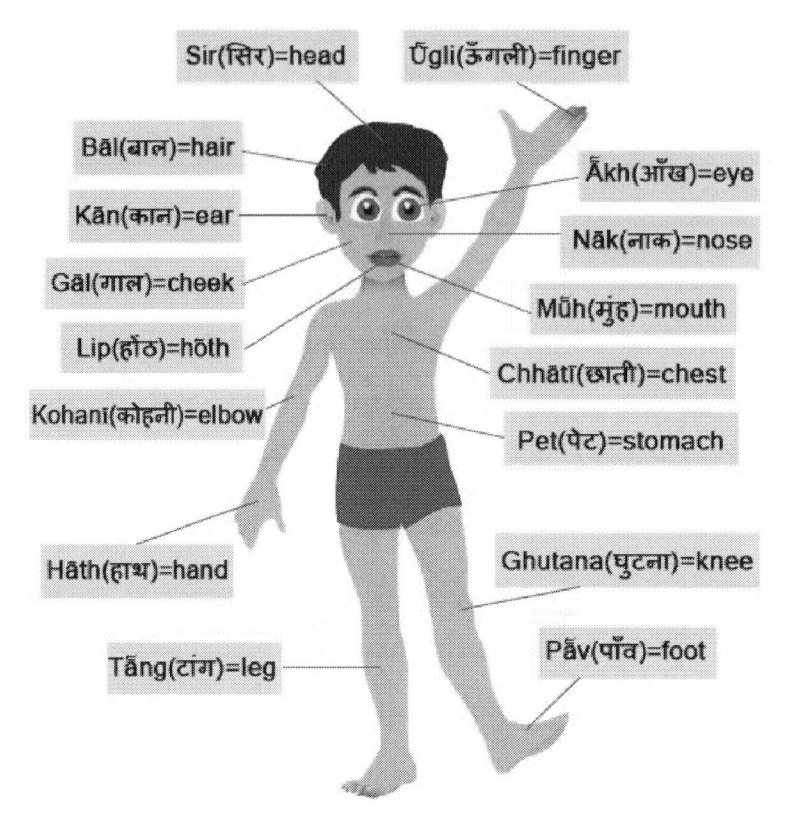

- Sir(सिर)=head
- Ůgli(ऊंगली)=finger
- Bāl(बाल)=hair
- Kān(कान)=ear
- Gāl(गाल)=cheek
- Lip(होंठ)=hōth
- Kohani(कोहनी)=elbow
- Hāth(हाथ)=hand
- Tāng(टांग)=leg
- Ãkh(आँख)=eye
- Nāk(नाक)=nose
- Mũh(मुंह)=mouth
- Chhātī(छाती)=chest
- Pet(पेट)=stomach
- Ghutana(घुटना)=knee
- Pẵv(पाँव)=foot

A good number of parts of the body are considered masculine. See the examples below:

English	Hindi	Devanagari
Ear	Kān	कान
Mouth	Mũh	मुँह
Lip	Hōth	होंठ
Hair	Bāl	बाल
Head	Sir	सिर
Foot	Pẵv	पाँव
Hand	Hāth	हाथ
Stomach	Pet	पेट
Cheek	Gāl	गाल
Knee	Ghutanā	घुटना

There are some exceptions to this rule. For example, the following parts of the body are considered feminine:

English	Hindi	Devanagari
Nose	Nāk	नाक
Eye	Ãkh	आँख
Finger	Ũglī	ऊँगली
Chest	Chhātī	छाती
Elbow	Kohanī	कोहनी
Leg	Tāng	टांग

Rule 5: Metals

A good number of metals are considered masculine. See the examples below:

- Iron = Lohā   लोहा
- Brass = Pītal   पीतल
- Copper = Tāmbā   तांबा

Rule 6: Miscellaneous

A good number of "oceans", "rocks", "mountains" and "grain" are considered masculine in Hindi. See the examples below:

Oceans

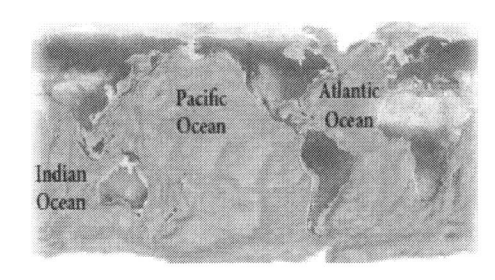

- Pacific Ocean = Prashãt Mahāsāgar प्रशांत महासागर
- Indian Ocean = Hĩd Mahāsāgar   हिंद महासागर

Rocks

- Pearl = Motī मोती
- Diamond = Hīrā हीरा

Mountains

- Himalaya = Himālay हिमालय
- Everest = Everest ऐवरेस्ट

Grain

- Wheat = Gehū̃ गेहूँ
- Rice = Chāwal चावल

Now, we will focus on basic rules for identifying feminine nouns.

Rules to determine feminine in Hindi

In this section, we will learn basic rules to identify feminine nouns in Hindi.

Rule 1: Gender of living things

This rule is straightforward and works exactly like other languages. Nouns that refer to females such as girl, mother, and aunt are considered "feminine".

English nouns (feminine)	Hindi nouns (feminine)	Devanagari
Girl	Ladkī	लड़की
Sister	Bahan	बहन
Sister-in-law	Bhābhī	भाभी
Daughter	Betī	बेटी
Mother	Mã	माँ
Grandmother (*maternal*)	Nānī	नानी
Grandmother (*paternal*)	Dādī	दादी
Aunt (*maternal*)	Māmī	मामी
Aunt (*paternal*)	Chāchī	चाची
Niece (Brother's daughter)	Bhatījī	भतीजी
Female horse	Ghodī	घोड़ी

Rule 2: Common nouns ending with the "ī" (ई)

This rule is similar to other languages where common nouns ending with "ī" are considered feminine.

English Nouns (feminine)	Hindi Nouns (feminine)	Devanagari
Bread	Rotī	रोटी
Girl	Ladkī	लड़की
Hat	Topī	टोपी
Letter	Chitthī	चिट्ठी
River	Nadī	नदी
Russian	Rūsī	रूसी

Rule 3: Nouns ending with "iyā" (ि◌या)

- Basket = Daliyā   डलिया
- Bird = Chidiyā   चिड़िया
- Doll = Gudiyā   गुड़िया

Rule 4: Some nouns ending with the "ta" (त) sound

- Chat = Bāt   बात
- Kick = Lāt   लात
- Night = Rāt   रात

Rule 5: Nouns ending with the "kha" (ख) sound

- Hunger = Bhūkh   भूख
- Scream = Chīkh   चीख

Rule 6: Nouns ending with the "at" (अट) sound

- Decoration = Sajāwat   सजावट
- Nausea = Gabrāhat   गबराहट
- Noise / Sound = Āhat   आहट

Rule 7: Miscellaneous

A good number of "rivers", "languages" and "food items" are considered feminine in Hindi. See the examples:

Rivers

- Ganges = Gãgā   गंगा
- Sarasvati = Saraswatī   सरस्वती
- Yamuna = Yamunā   यमुना

Languages

- Hindi = Hindī   हिन्दी
- English = Ãgrezī   अंग्रेज़ी
- French = Phrench   फ्रेंच

Food Items

- Lentil soup = Dāl   दाल
- Kachori = Kachorī   कचोरी
- Vegetable = Sabzī   सब्जी

Exercise 2.1 Help Pingu categorize the following nouns as *feminine* or *masculine*

chittī	tel	bhūkh	Himālaya	bachpan	darwāzā	ā̃kh
nānī	hāth	lohā	Gã̄gā	rāt	gudiyā	sabjī	lagāv
Spanish	betā	sajāwat	gehū̃	hīrā	Hind mahāsāgar

Feminine:
_____

Masculine:
_____

Watch the video "Masculine and Feminine" at YouTube.com/HindiUniversity (playlist: Pingu Learns To Speak Hindi) to deepen your learning.

Hindi Vocabulary

Review the following vocabulary words with Pingu and learn their gender classification.

Masculine			Feminine		
English	Hindī	Devanagari	English	Hindī	Devanagari
Grandfather (mom's side)	Nānā	नाना	Grandmother (mom's side)	Nānī	नानी
Grandfather (dad's side)	Dādā	दादा	Grandmother (dad's side)	Dādī	दादी
Door	Darwāzā	दरवाज़ा	Language	Bhāshā	भाषा
Siblings	Bhāī Bahan	भाई बहन	Journey, travel	Yātrā	यात्रा
Childhood	Bachpan	बचपन	Story	Kahānī	कहानी
Neighbour	Padosī	पड़ोसी	Female friend	Sahelī	सहेली
Mountain	Parvat	पर्वत	River	Nadī	नदी
Tree	Ped	पेड़	Pen	Kalam	क़लम
Pillow	Takiyā	तकिया	Book	Kitāb	किताब
Money	Rupaye	रुपए	Job	Naukrī	नौकरी
Friend	Dost	दोस्त	Watch	Ghadī	घड़ी
Address	Patā	पता	Hat	Topī	टोपी
Glasses	Chashmā	चश्मा	Table	Mez	मेज़
Shoe	Jūtā	जूता	Bottle	Shīshī	शीशी
Bed	Palang	पलंग	Window	Khidkī	खिड़की
Apple	Seb	सेब	Chair	Kursī	कुर्सी
Cloth	Kapdā	कपड़ा	Doll	Gudiyā	गुड़िया
House	Ghar	घर	Tea	Chāy	चाय

Formula 2

It's challenging for Pingu to determine if a given noun is masculine or feminine, especially for non-living objects.

To make this a bit easier, I have created some formulae. These formulae are written in Hindi and allow us to clarify if the noun is masculine or feminine.

Here we go:

- Kyā Hindī mẽ _____ masculine hai?
- क्या हिन्दी में _____ masculine है ?

So let's say if Pingu doesn't know the gender of the word for tree and river, she can use the formula.

- Kyā Hindī mẽ __ ped__ masculine hai? (Is 'tree' masculine in Hindi?)
- क्या हिन्दी में पेड़ masculine है ?

- Kyā Hindī mẽ __ nadī__ masculine hai?
- क्या हिन्दी में नदी masculine है ?

The person you are speaking with will gladly tell you the answer:

- Hā̃, __ped__ masculine hai. (Yes, "tree" is masculine.)
- हाँ, पेड़ masculine है ।

- Nahī̃, __ nadī__ masculine nahī̃ hai. (No, "river" is not masculine.)
- नहीं, नदी masculine नहीं है ।

You might get weird looks when you use this formula (Kyā Hindī mẽ _____ masculine hai?), not because it's incorrect, but they will think why are you asking this. This is a language learning hack I came up with in the last 10+ years of teaching.

Get inspired by HindiUniversity students

Provided below are some excellent excerpts from essays by the students of the HindiUniversity.

Saida (Morocco)

Namaste dostõ, merā nām Saida hai. Maĩ Morocco se hũ. Maĩ ek saleswoman hũ. Merī umr battīs sāl hai. Mujhe bhārat kī purānī jagahẽ bahut pasand haĩ. Āpse milkar khushī huī.

नमस्ते दोस्तों , मेरा नाम Saida है । मैं Morocco से हूँ । मैं एक saleswoman हूँ । मेरी उम्र बत्तीस साल है । मुझे भारत की पुरानी जगहें बहुत पसंद हैं । आपसे मिलकर ख़ुशी हुई ।

Edith (Mexico)

Merā nām Edith hai. maĩ Mexico se hũ. maĩ atthāis sāl kī hũ. Maĩ Hindī padh rahī hũ. Mujhe Hindī bahut acchī lagtī hai, mujhe chocolates acchī lagtī haĩ. Maĩ Hindī sīkhnā chāhtī hũ kyõ ki ek din maĩ Bhārat jāũgī.

मेरा नाम Edith है । मैं Mexico से हूँ । मैं अट्ठाइस साल की हूँ । मैं हिन्दी पढ़ रही हूँ। मुझे हिन्दी बहुत अच्छी लगती है, मुझे chocolates अच्छी लगती हैं । मैं हिन्दी सीखना चाहती हूँ क्यों कि एक दिन मैं भारत जाऊँगी ।

Kevin (Ontario)

Merā nām Kevin hai aur maĩ Ontario mẽ rehtā hũ. Mere sabse acche dost kā nām Ady hai. Ady ke pās ek sundar gadī hai. Gadī kā rang harā hai. Ady kā ghar jungal ke pās hai aur bahut badā hai. Vah kitābẽ likhtā hai. Ady kī kitābẽ bahut mazedār haĩ. Ady ke ladke bhī kahāniyā̃ likhte haĩ.

मेरा नाम Kevin है और मैं Ontario में रहता हूँ । मेरे सबसे अच्छे दोस्त का नाम Ady है । Ady के पास एक सुंदर गाड़ी है । गाड़ी का रंग हरा है । Ady का घर जंगल के पास है और बहुत बड़ा है । वह किताबें लिखता है । Ady की किताबें बहुत मज़ेदार हैं । Ady के लड़के भी कहानियाँ लिखते हैं ।

Chapter 3
Penguin vs. Penguins In Hindi

+ Pingu will learn about Hindi singular and plurals. She will also learn about relationships in Hindi, i.e., Pingu's mother, Pingu's brother, etc.

Number

Number is an important concept in Hindi. Learning the proper forms: Singular or Plural will help you conjugate verbs, adjectives, post-positions correctly. In this chapter, you will learn rules for Hindi singular/plural. First, you will learn about rules for masculine nouns, then for feminine nouns.

Plural form of Masculine Nouns

Let's first discuss how the singular/plural works for the masculine nouns. Masculine nouns can be categorized further as Marked and Unmarked nouns.

Masculine Nouns	
Marked Nouns	**Unmarked Nouns**
• Marked nouns end with "ā" • When you make the noun plural, the ending changes to the "e" sound.	• All other masculine nouns which do not end with "ā" • When you make the noun plural, the ending does not change.

Marked Nouns

As shown in the table above, the ending of masculine "marked nouns" often change from "ā" to "e" sound when making a noun plural.

Singular			Plural		
Betā	बेटा	Son	Bete	बेटे	Sons
Kamrā	कमरा	Room	Kamre	कमरे	Rooms
Kelā	केला	Banana	Kele	केले	Bananas
Ladkā	लड़का	Boy	Ladke	लड़के	Boys
Santarā	संतरा	Orange	Santare	संतरे	Oranges

Exercise 3.1 Help Pingu change the following nouns into plural.

1　Chehrā चेहरा (face): _____
2　Māthā माथा (forehead): _____
3　Topā टोपा (hat): _____
4　Lotā लोटा (vessel): _____

Unmarked Nouns

These nouns keep the same form when you change them to plural.

Singular			Plural		
Ādmī	आदमी	Man	Ādmī	आदमी	Men
Akhbār	अख़बार	Newspaper	Akhbār	अख़बार	Newspapers
Ghar	घर	House	Ghar	घर	Houses
Shehar	शहर	City	Shehar	शहर	Cities

Exercise 3.2 Help Pingu change the following unmarked nouns into plural.

1　Phone फ़ोन (phone): _____
2　Bāl बाल (hair): _____
3　Hāth हाथ (hand): _____
4　Kāgaz काग़ज़ (paper): _____

Watch the video "Hindi Singular vs Plural" from YouTube.com/HindiUniversity (playlist: Pingu Learns To Speak Hindi) to deepen your learning.

Plural form of Feminine Nouns

Now let's discuss how the singular/plural works for the feminine nouns. Similar to masculine nouns, feminine nouns can also be classified as Marked and Unmarked nouns.

Feminine Nouns	
Marked Nouns	**Unmarked Nouns**
<ul><li>Marked nouns end with "ī"</li><li>When you make a noun plural, the ending changes to "iyā̃."</li></ul>	<ul><li>Not ending with "ī"</li><li>When you make a noun plural, the ending changes to "ẽ."</li></ul>

Marked Nouns

When you make plurals, the ending of feminine "marked nouns" often changes from "ī" to "iyā̃" ियाँ .

Singular			Plural		
Betī	बेटी	Daughter	Betiyā̃	बेटियाँ	Daughters
Ladkī	लड़की	Girl	Ladkiyā̃	लड़कियाँ	Girls
Mithāī	मिठाई	Sweet	Mithāiyā̃	मिठाइयाँ	Sweets
Sārī	साड़ी	Sari	Sāriyā̃	साड़ियाँ	Saris
Gādī	गाड़ी	Car	Gādiyā̃	गाड़ियाँ	Cars
Billī	बिल्ली	Cat	Billiyā̃	बिल्लियाँ	Cats

Exercise 3.3 Help Pingu change the following nouns into plural.

1. Devī देवी (goddess): _____
2. Dawāī दवाई (medicine): _____
3. Rajāī रजाई (blanket): _____
4. Kaḍāhī कड़ाही (cooking pot): _____

Unmarked Nouns

When you make plurals, we add "ẽ" ऍ sound to the ending of feminine "unmarked nouns."

Singular			Plural		
Aurat	औरत	Woman	Auratẽ	औरतें	Women
Bā̃h	बाँह	Arm	Bā̃hẽ	बाँहें	Arms
Kitāb	किताब	Book	Kitābẽ	किताबें	Books
Rāt	रात	Night	Rātẽ	रातें	Nights

Exercise 3.4 Help Pingu change the following unmarked nouns into plural.

1. Bahan बहन (sister): _____
2. Ā̃kh आँख (eye): _____
3. Bāt बात (thing): _____
4. Mez मेज़ (table): _____

> Watch the video "Hindi Singular vs. Plural" from YouTube.com/HindiUniversity (playlist: Pingu Learns To Speak Hindi) to deepen your learning.

Exercise 3.5 Help Piungu write the gender, the singular, and plural form of the objects below. You can use the vocabulary in chapter 2 for reference.

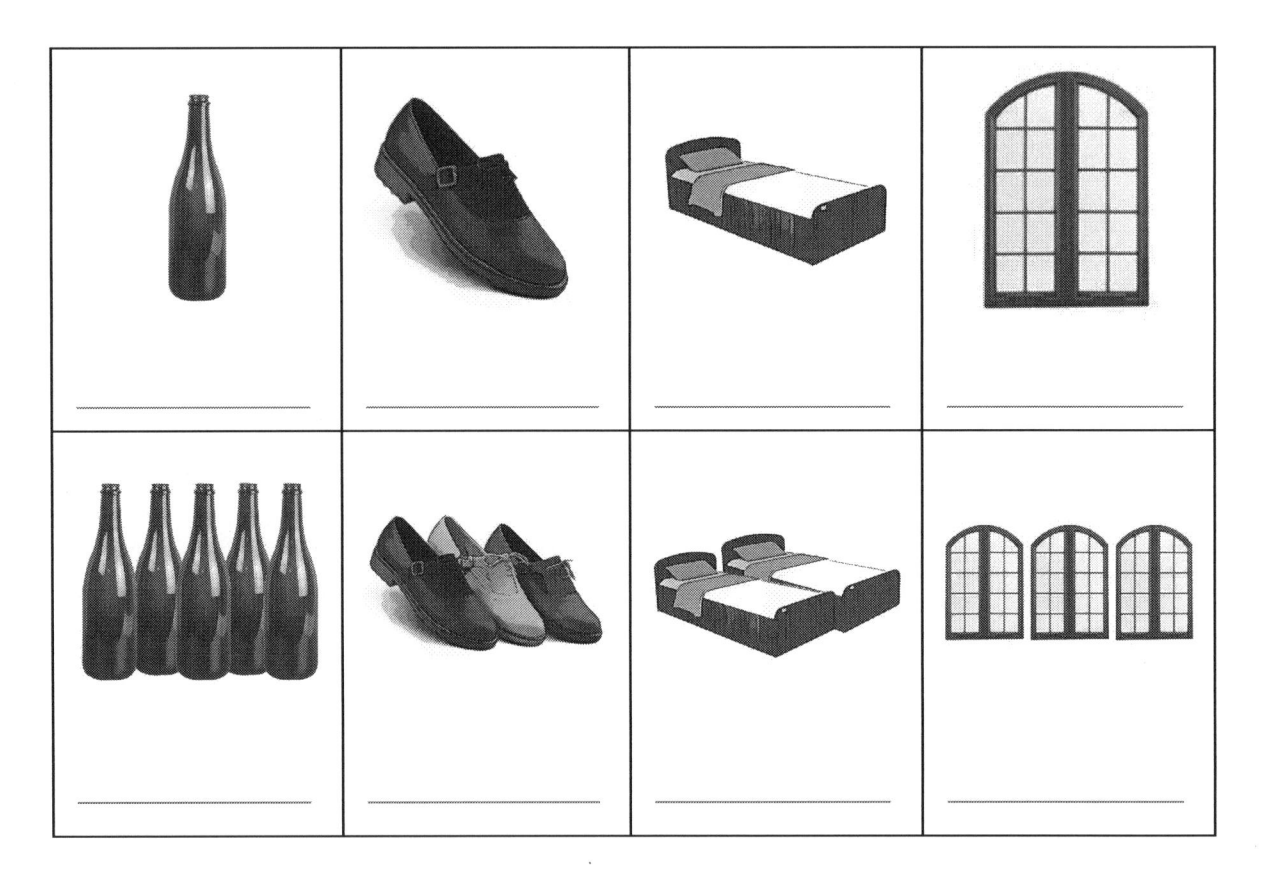

Kā/Kī and Ke (का/की and के)

In chapter 1, we focused on two postpositions, "Se" & "Mẽ." In this chapter, I want to introduce three more Hindi postpositions: Kā, Kī, and Ke.

- These postpositions (Kā, Kī, and Ke) define the relationship between nouns/pronouns with (other) nouns that follow them.
- They also denote possession & relationship.
- In English, this relationship is often represented using an apostrophe s ('s) i.e., Ram's, John's, etc.

Let's see how to use them:

Using "Kā" (का) in Hindi

The postposition Kā defines the relationship between nouns/pronouns with the singular masculine noun that comes after it.

English	Hindi	Devanagari
Pingu's brother	Pingu kā bhāī	Pingu का भाई
Tom's son	Tom kā ladkā	Tom का लड़का
Mary's brother	Mary kā bhāī	Mary का भाई
Yhon's laptop	Yhon kā laptop	Yhon का laptop
Jason's bag	Jason kā bag	Jason का bag
Sarah's college	Sarah kā college	Sarah का college

A few things to notice here:

- **Pingu kā bhāī (brother)**, Kā is used to show the relationship between Pingu and his brother.
- Kā is used here because bhāī (brother) is considered singular masculine.
- You use Kā /Kī and Ke based on the gender of "thing" possessed by the subject (i.e., the gender of brother, son, etc.)
    - Subject - Sarah (feminine in Hindi)
    - Since "college" is masculine, we will use Kā to show the relationship between Sarah and her college.

Exercise 3.6 Help Pingu translate the following sentences in Hindi.

1. Bob's lunch: _____
2. Alicia's coat: _____
3. Mia's husband: _____
4. Sam's pen: _____

Hint: Look at the gender of lunch, coat, husband, and pen.

Using "Ke" (के) in Hindi

Similarly, when the "thing" possessed by the subject is *masculine plural*, you will be using "Ke" to denote the relationship between the subject and the "thing" possessed by the subject.

English	Hindi	Devanagari
Pingu's relatives	Pingu ke relatives	Pingu के relatives
Tom's sons	Tom ke ladke	Tom के लड़के
Yhon's laptops	Yhon ke laptops	Yhon के laptops
Jason's bags	Jason ke bags	Jason के bags
Sarah's colleges	Sarah ke colleges	Sarah के colleges

Exercise 3.7 Help Pingu translate the following sentences in Hindi.

1. Pingu's parents: _____
2. Alicia's coats: _____
3. Mia's clothes: _____
4. Sam's shoes: _____

Using "Kī" (की) in Hindi

Now that we have learned kā and ke, let's discuss how to use kī in sentences. As you might have guessed, when the "thing" possessed by the subject is "feminine singular" or "feminine plural," you will be using kī to denote the relationship between them.

English	Hindi	Devanagari
Pingu's mom	Pingu kī mā̃	Pingu की माँ
Tom's daughter	Tom kī ladkī	Tom की लड़की
Yhon's watch	Yhon kī ghadī	Yhon की घड़ी
Jason's key	Jason kī chābī	Jason की चाबी
Sarah's car	Sarah kī gādī	Sarah की गाड़ी

In the table above, daughter, sister, watch, key, and bike are considered feminine singular in Hindi. Now, let's see examples of when the object is "feminine plural."

English	Hindi	Devanagari
Pingu's girlfriends	Pingu kī saheliyā̃	Pingu की सहेलियाँ
Tom's daughters	Tom kī ladkiyā̃	Tom की लड़कियाँ
Yhon's watches	Yhon kī ghadiyā̃	Yhon की घड़ियाँ
Jason's keys	Jason kī chābiyā̃	Jason की चाबियाँ
Sarah's cars	Sarah kī gādiyā̃	Sarah की गाड़ियाँ
Sarah's responsibilities	Sarah kī jimmerdāriyā̃	Sarah की जिम्मेदारियाँ

Exercise 3.8 Help Pingu translate the following sentences in Hindi.

1 Bob's problems: _____

2 Alicia's saris: _____

3 Mia's weaknesses: _____

Exercise 3.9 Using the postposition Kā/Kī and Ke, help Pingu make Hindi sentences that show the relationship between Lia/David and the things they possess (i.e., Lia's glasses, David's books).

Maĩ Lia hū̃.
मैं Liya हूँ ।

Maĩ David hū̃.
मैं David हूँ ।

Hint: To use kā/kī/ke correctly, you will have to select things that belong to Lia and David. You can use the vocabulary table in chapter 2 to find the gender of the words.

Watch the video "Hindi Postposition" at YouTube.com/HindiUniversity (playlist: Pingu Learns To Speak Hindi) to deepen your learning and help turn insight into action.

Formula 3

As a beginner, it is hard to memorize the plural of all Hindi nouns. You can use the formula below to help with this.

Here we go:

- What is the plural of _____ ?
- _____ kā bahuvachan (plural) kyā hai?
- _____ का बहुवचन क्या है ?

Let's say if you don't know the Hindi plural for "kitāb" (book).

- Kitāb kā bahuvachan (plural) kyā hai?
- You will likely get a response Kitābẽ.

- Nadī (River) kā bahuvachan (plural) kyā hai?
- You will likely get a response Nadiyã (Rivers).

Get inspired by HindiUniversity students

Cecilia (Romania)

Merā nām Cecilia hai. Maī Romania se hū̃. Mere ghar mē do kamre haī. Pehle kamre mē, do palang, do mezē, tīn kursiyā̃ aur do almāriyā̃ haī. Yah kamrā bahut havādār hai kyõki khidkiyā̃ badī haī. Dūsre kamre mē, sirf ek kursī aur ek palang hai. Bagīce mē tīn bade ped aur ek chotā ped haī. Ek bade ped ke nīche ek mez aur chār kursiyā̃ haī.

मेरा नाम Cecilia है । मैं Romania से हूँ । मेरे घर में दो कमरे हैं । पहले कमरे में, दो पलंग, दो मेज़ें, तीन कुर्सियाँ और दो अलमारियाँ हैं । यह कमरा बहुत हवादार है क्योंकि खिड़कियाँ बड़ी हैं । दूसरे कमरे में, सिर्फ एक कुर्सी और एक पलंग हैं । बगीचे में तीन बड़े पेड़ और एक छोटा पेड़ हैं । एक बड़े पेड़ के नीचे एक मेज़ और चार कुर्सियाँ हैं।

Tara (Iran)

Merā nām Tara hai. Mere ghar ke pās ek skul hai. Is school mē tīn manjilē haī. Har manjil mē chhah kakshāē haī. Har kakshā mē 12 bench haī. Har kakshā mē ek mez, ek kursī aur ek board hai. is school mē bahut sāre chhātr haī aur sabhī chhātr bahut ūrjāvān haī. merī do chhotī bahanē bhī is school kī chhātr haī.

मेरा नाम Tara है। मेरे घर के पास एक स्कूल है । इस स्कूल में तीन मंजिलें हैं । हर मंजिल में छह कक्षाएँ हैं । हर कक्षा में 12 बेंच हैं । हर कक्षा में एक मेज़, एक कुर्सी और एक बोर्ड है । इस स्कूल में बहुत सारे छात्र हैं और सभी छात्र बहुत ऊर्जावान हैं । मेरी दो छोटी बहनें भी इस स्कूल की छात्र हैं।

Crystal (Missouri, USA)

Merā nām Crystal hai. Mujhko kitābē bahut pasand haī. Mere ghar ke pīche ek sundar bagīchā hai. Bagīce mē tīn ped, ek mez aur chār kursiyā̃ haī. Maī har dopahar ko bagīche mē ek kitāb padhtī hū̃. Mere do kutte aur ek billī haī. Bagīche mē unke do chote ghar haī. Ve bahut khush haī !

मेरा नाम Crystal है । मुझको किताबें बहुत पसंद हैं । मेरे घर के पीछे एक सुंदर बगीचा है । बगीचे में तीन पेड़ , एक मेज़ और चार कुर्सियाँ हैं । मैं हर दोपहर को बगीचे में एक किताब पढ़ती हूँ । मेरे दो कुत्ते और एक बिल्ली हैं । बगीचे में उनके दो छोटे घर हैं । वे बहुत खुश हैं !

Chapter 4

Hindi Pronouns

+ Pingu will learn to use various Hindi pronouns and form simple Hindi sentences.

Personal Pronouns (I, You, We, They, he, she, it)

A personal pronoun is a pronoun that is associated primarily with a particular person in the grammatical sense. We learned a personal pronoun "Maĩ" in chapter 1, which means "I". In this section, we will be covering a few more personal pronouns.

English	Hindi	Devanagari
I	Maĩ	मैं
You (familiar)	Tum	तुम
You (intimate)	Tū	तू
He / She / It	Vah / Yah	वह / यह
We	Hum	हम
You (formal)	Āp	आप
They	Ye/ Ve	ये/ वे

Please review the sentences we covered in chapter #1 using "Maĩ".

In English, you will form basic sentences, such as:

- I am _____
- You are _____
- He/She is _____
- We are _____
- You are _____
- They are _____

In this case, "am", "are" and "is" are all forms of the verb "to be." We have something similar in Hindi. The table below shows Hindi forms of the verb "to be" for respective "personal pronouns".

English	Hindi	Devanagari
I am ____ .	Maĩ ____ hũ.	मैं ____ हूँ ।
You are ____ (familiar).	Tum ____ ho.	तुम ____ हो ।
You are ____ (intimate)	Tū ____ hai..	तू ____ है ।
He/She is ____ .	Vah ____ hai.	वह ____ है ।
We are ____ .	Hum ____ haĩ.	हम ____ हैं ।
You are ____ (formal)	Āp ____ haĩ.	आप ____ हैं ।
They are ____ .	Ve ____ haĩ.	वे ____ हैं ।

Let's add some objects in these constructs and have fun making small Hindi sentences.

- I am a student.
  - Maĩ student hũ.
  - मैं student हूँ ।

- You (familiar) are a student.
  - Tum student ho.
  - तुम student हो ।

- You (intimate) are a student.
  - Tū student hai.
  - तू student है ।

- He is a student.
  - Vah student hai.
  - वह student है ।

- We are students.
  - Hum students haĩ.
  - हम students हैं ।

- You are a student.
  - Āp student haĩ.
  - आप student हैं ।

- They are students.
  - Ve students haĩ.
  - वे students हैं ।

Exercise 4.1 Help Pingu complete the following sentences and write their meaning.

1 Maĩ khush _____ .   १ मैं खुश _____ ।
2 Āp kahā̃ _____ ?   २ आप कहाँ _____ ?
3 Hum french _____ .   ३ हम french _____ ।
4 Vah engineer _____ .   ४ वह engineer _____ ।
5 Ve bacche _____ .   ५ वे बच्चे _____ ।

Exercise 4.2 Help Pingu say the following sentences in Hindi

1 I am a traveler.
2 She is American.
3 We are scientists.
4 They are vegetarian.
5 You are amazing.
6 He is tall.
7 She is upset.

Exercise 4.3 Translate the following Hindi sentences in your native language.

1 Ve nārāz haĩ.   १ वे नाराज़ हैं ।
2 Vah artist hai.   २ वह artist है ।
3 Hum pareshān haĩ   ३ हम परेशान हैं ।
4 Maĩ Lisa hū̃.   ४ मैं Lisa हूँ ।
5 Āp patrakār haĩ.   ५ आप पत्रकार हैं ।

Exercise 4.4 Help Pingu read the following paragraph and prepare something similar for her.

"Maĩ ek artist hū̃. Maĩ France se hū̃. Maĩ downtown Paris mẽ rehtā hū̃. Yah painting $5000 kī hai. Yah Europe kī unique painting hai aur 200 sāl purāni hai".

मैं एक artist हूँ। मैं France से हूँ । मैं downtown Paris में रहता हूँ । यह painting $5000 की है । यह Europe की unique painting है और 200 साल पुरानी है ।

Demonstrative Pronouns

A demonstrative pronoun is a pronoun used to point to something specific within a sentence. In English, demonstrative pronouns are *this, that, these, and those*. These pronouns can indicate items in space or time, and they can be either singular or plural.

Let's learn third person pronouns in Hindi.

Demonstrative Pronouns	
Hindi	**English**
Yah यह	This
Vah वह	That
Ye ये	These
Ve वे	Those

In English, you will form basic sentences as:

- This is _____ .
- That is _____ .
- These are _____ .
- Those are _____ .

In this case, "is" and "are" are considered forms of the verb "to be." In Hindi, we have something similar. The table below shows the Hindi forms of the verb "to be" for the respective "demonstrative pronoun.".

Hindi	English	Rule
This is _____ .	Yah _____ hai.	Used with singular nouns.
That is _____ .	Vah _____ hai.	
These are _____ .	Ye _____ haĩ.	Used with plural nouns.
Those are _____ .	Ve _____ haĩ.	

Ready to start making some sentences in Hindi?

- This is a room.
  - Yah kamrā hai.
  - यह कमरा है।

- This is a pen.
  - Yah kalam hai.
  - यह क़लम है।

- That is a school.
  - Vah school hai.
  - वह school है।

- That is a river.
  - Vah nadī hai.
  - वह नदी है।

- These are rooms.
  - Ye kamre haĩ.
  - ये कमरे हैं।

- These are cars.
  - Ye gāḍiyā̃ haĩ.
  - ये गाड़ियाँ हैं।

- Those are boxes.
  - Ve dabbe haĩ.
  - वे डिब्बे हैं।

- Those are ships.
  - Ve jahāz haĩ.
  - वे जहाज़ हैं।

Exercise 4.5 Help Pingu translate the following sentences into Hindi.

1. This is a watch. _____
2. Those are hats. _____
3. These are my friends. _____
4. That is my address. _____

Exercise 4.6 Read the following Hindi sentences. Can you write their meaning in your native language?

1. Yah merī bhāshā haĩ. (यह मेरी भाषा है।) _____
2. Vah merā bhāī haĩ. (वह मेरा भाई है।) _____
3. Ye kapde haĩ. (ये कपड़े हैं।) _____
4. Ve vidyārthī (students) haĩ. (वे विद्यार्थी हैं।) _____

Possessive Pronouns

Possessive pronouns are words used to indicate that something belongs to someone or has a direct relationship with someone else. In this section will learn possessive pronouns like *my, yours, ours, his, her, and theirs*.

Possessive pronouns are formed when *personal pronouns* are used along with the post-positions *kā / kī / ke*. Let's review them in the table below.

Pronouns form with post-positions kā / kī / ke			
Pronoun	**Post-position**	**Outcome**	**English**
Maĩ	kā / kī / ke	merā / merī / mere	My
Tū		terā / terī / tere	Your
Tum		tumhārā / tumhārī / tumhāre	Your
Vah		uskā / uskī / uske	His / Her
Yah		iskā / iskī / iske	His / Her
Āp		āpkā / āpkī / āpke	Your
Hum		humārā / humārī / humāre	Our
Ye		inkā / inkī / inke	Their
Ve		unkā / unkī / unke	Their

Watch "Possessive Pronoun - 1" & "Possessive Pronoun - 2" at YouTube.com/HindiUniversity to deepen your learning.

Ready to start making some sentences in Hindi?

- My room
  - Merā kamrā (masculine singular)
  - मेरा कमरा

- Your car
  - Terī gāḍī (feminine singular)
  - तेरी गाड़ी

- Our children
  - Humāre bacche (masculine plural)
  - हमारे बच्चे

- Her book
  - Uskī kitābẽ (feminine plural)
  - उसकी किताबें

- His garden
  - Uskā bagīchā (masculine singular)
  - उसका बगीचा

- Their sons
  - Unke bete (masculine plural)
  - उनके बेटे

- Your daughters
  - Āpkī betiyā̃ (feminine plural)
  - आपकी बेटियाँ

- My hat
  - Merī topī (feminine singular)
  - मेरी टोपी

Exercise 4.7. Help Pingu translate the following sentences into Hindi.

1. This is our house.
2. That is my brother.
3. She is my sister.
4. They are his friends.
5. He is your teacher. (formal)
6. Their car is big.
7. This is your book.
8. Her room is small.
9. My daughter is married.
10. Your son is healthy. (intimate)

Hindi Vocabulary

English	Hindi	Devanagari
Room	Kamrā	कमरा
Car	Gāḍī	गाड़ी
Box	Dibbā	डिब्बा
Ship	Jahāz	जहाज़
Where	Kahā̃	कहाँ
Children	Bacche	बच्चे
Upset	Nārāz	नाराज़
Artist	Kalākār	कलाकार
Upset	Pareshān	परेशान
Mom	Mā̃	माँ
Journalist	Patrakār	पत्रकार
Songwriter	Gītkār	गीतकार
Student	Vidhyārtī	विद्यार्थी

Get inspired by HindiUniversity students

Cecilia (Romania)

Namaste! Merā nām Cecilia hai aur maĩ ek kalākār hū̃. Mere do bacche haĩ, ek ladkī aur ek ladkā. Ve vidyārthī haĩ aur unkā vidyālay humāre ghar ke pās hai. Hum ek sundar ghar mẽ rehte haĩ. Humārā ek kuttā hai. Vah har din uske khilaunõ ke sāth kheltā haĩ. Āj vah nārāz hai kyõ ki hamāre pās uske liye samay nahī̃ haĩ.

नमस्ते ! मेरा नाम Cecilia है और मैं एक कलाकार हूँ । मेरे दो बच्चे हैं, एक लड़की और एक लड़का । वे विद्यार्थी हैं और उनका विद्यालय हमारे घर के पास है । हम एक सुंदर घर में रहते हैं । हमारा एक कुत्ता है। वह हर दिन उसके खिलौनों के साथ खेलता है । आज वह नाराज़ है क्यों कि हमारे पास उसके लिए समय नहीं हैं ।

Tara (Iran)

Merā nām Tara hai aur maĩ ek adhyāpikā hū̃. Maĩ apne parivār ke sāh ek bade shehar mẽ rehtī hū̃. Merī bahan kā nām Parvin hai. vah ek daftar mẽ kām kartī hai. Uskā daftar ghar se dūr hai. Humārā ghar chhotā hai lekin humārā bagīchā bahut sundar hai. Humāre padosī har saptāhā̃t humāre bagīche mẽ āte haĩ. Unke bagīche bahut chhote haĩ. Hum bahut lucky haĩ !

मेरा नाम Tara है और मैं एक अध्यापिका हूँ । मैं अपने परिवार के साथ एक बड़े शहर में रहती हूँ । मेरी बहन का नाम Parvin है । वह एक दफ्तर में काम करती है । उसका दफ्तर घर से दूर है । हमारा घर छोटा है लेकिन हमारा बगीचा बहुत सुंदर है । हमारे पड़ोसी हर सप्ताहांत हमारे बगीचे में आते हैं। उनके बगीचे बहुत छोटे हैं । हम बहुत lucky हैं !

Chapter 5
Pingu's daily routine

+ Pingu will learn to talk about her daily routine in Antarctica and learn to form sentences in the present indefinite tense.

Present Indefinite Tense

In this chapter, my goal is to provide you with tools to discuss your daily routine in Hindi. To do that, you will have to learn some personal pronouns and Hindi verbs. I recommend that you memorize the verbs' infinitive forms (e.g., to go, to drink, to eat). In Hindi, such verbs end with a "nā" ना sound (i.e., Jānā जाना, Pīnā पीना, Khānā खाना). In the first section of the book, you will learn the most common Hindi verbs.

Hindi Verbs

Now that you have mastered the use of personal pronouns and can form basic sentences, your next challenge is to learn commonly used Hindi verbs. I highly recommend that you memorize the following verbs.

Verb (infinitive form)		
English	**Hindi**	**Devanagari**
To be	Honā	होना
To buy	Kharīdnā	खरीदना
To cook	Pakānā	पकाना
To cry	Ronā	रोना
To dance	Nāchnā	नाचना
To do	Karnā	करना
To drink	Pīnā	पीना
To eat	Khānā	खाना
To fly	Udnā	उड़ना
To give	Denā	देना

To hear	Sunnā	सुनना
To jump	Kūdnā	कूदना
To know	Jānnā	जानना
To laugh	Hāsnā	हँसना
To learn	Sīknā	सीखना
To make	Banānā	बनाना
To read	Padhnā	पढ़ना
To see	Dekhnā	देखना
To sit	Baithnā	बैठना
To sleep	Sonā	सोना
To speak	Bolnā	बोलना
To swim	Tairnā	तैरना
To take	Lenā	लेना
To think	Sochnā	सोचना
To touch	Chūnā	छूना
To travel	Ghūmnā	घूमना
To understand	Samajhnā	समझना
To walk	Chalnā	चलना
To want	Chāhnā	चाहना
To wash	Dhonā	धोना
To write	Likhnā	लिखना

Watch the video "Hindi Verbs" at YouTube.com/HindiUniversity (playlist: Pingu Learns To Speak Hindi) to deepen your learning.

Present Indefinite Tense - Affirmative Sentences

In this section, you will use the concepts we just learned (personal pronouns and verbs) and form basic sentences. For example:

- I walk.
- You walk.
- He/She walks.
- We walk.
- You walk.
- They walk.

You may have noticed that verb conjugation is straightforward in English, as the verb remains the same for most of the pronouns (I, we, they, you) and changes only for he/she/it. This is because English is considered a "moderately inflected" language. In contrast, Hindi is regarded as a "highly inflected" language, and the verbs are conjugated (i.e., modified) based on the pronouns.

Let's review the rules for verb conjugation. The verb used here is "Chalnā", which means "*to walk*". You will notice "na" in the verb gets replaced based on the pronoun.

Subject	Verb Conjugation (Chalnā)	Rules
Maĩ	Chaltā *(male)* hũ. Chaltī *(female)* hũ.	Replace "nā" in the verb with "tā" for the masculine singular pronoun. Replace "nā" in the verb with "tī" for the feminine singular pronoun.
Tum	Chalte *(male)* ho. Chaltī *(female)* ho.	Replace "nā" in the verb with "te". Replace "nā" in the verb with "tī".
Tū Vah / Yah	Chaltā *(male)* hai. Chaltī *(female)* hai.	Replace "nā" in the verb with "tā". Replace "nā" in the verb with "tī".
Hum Āp Ve / Ye	Chalte *(male)* haĩ. Chaltī *(female)* haĩ.	Replace "nā" in the verb with "te". Replace "nā" in the verb with "tī".

In the scenarios above, we have replaced "nā" with "tā", "te" or "tī" based on the pronoun. Thus, "chalnā" is modified into "chaltā", "chalte" and "chaltī".

So our sentences will look like this:

- I walk.
    - Maĩ chaltā hū̃. *(male)*
    - मैं चलता हूँ ।

- I walk.
    - Maĩ chaltī hū̃. *(female)*
    - मैं चलती हूँ ।

- You (familiar) walk.
    - Tum chalte ho. *(male)*
    - तुम चलते हो ।

- You (intimate) walk.
    - Tū chaltā hai. *(male)*
    - तू चलता है ।

- He walks.
    - Vah chaltā hai.
    - वह चलता है ।

- She walks.
    - Vah chaltī hai.
    - वह चलती है ।

- We walk.
    - Hum chalte haĩ.
    - हम चलते हैं ।

- You walk.
    - Āp chalte haĩ.
    - आप चलते हैं ।

- They walk.
    - Ve chalte haĩ.
    - वे चलते हैं ।

Watch the video "Present Indefinite Tense" at YouTube.com/HindiUniversity (playlist: Pingu Learns To Speak Hindi) to deepen your learning.

Exercise 5.1 Help Pingu complete the following sentences with the right verb conjugation.

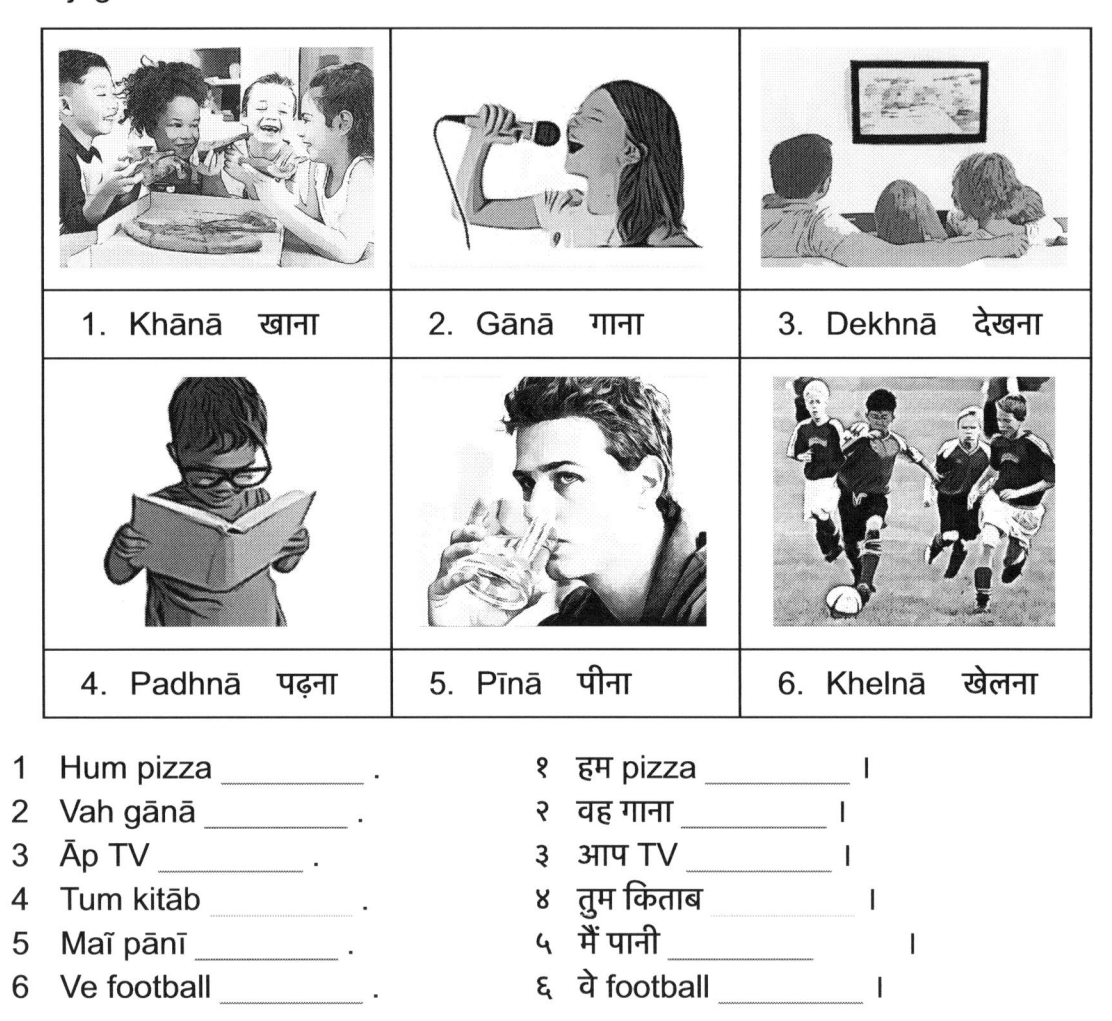

1. Khānā खाना	2. Gānā गाना	3. Dekhnā देखना
4. Padhnā पढ़ना	5. Pīnā पीना	6. Khelnā खेलना

1 Hum pizza _____ .
2 Vah gānā _____ .
3 Āp TV _____ .
4 Tum kitāb _____ .
5 Maĩ pānī _____ .
6 Ve football _____ .

१ हम pizza _____ ।
२ वह गाना _____ ।
३ आप TV _____ ।
४ तुम किताब _____ ।
५ मैं पानी _____ ।
६ वे football _____ ।

Exercise 5.2 Help Pingu choose the correct verb in the sentences below.

Sonā   bolnā   dekhnā   khelnā   gānā   pīnā

1 Maĩ India mẽ cricket _____ .
2 Ve subah chāy _____ .
3 Hum french _____ .
4 Āp samay pe _____ .
5 Vah har din bhajan _____ . *(male)*
6 Vah Bollywood film _____ . *(female)*

१ मैं India में cricket _____ ।
२ वे सुबह चाय _____ ।
३ हम french _____ ।
४ आप समय पे _____ ।
५ वह हर दिन भजन _____ ।
६ वह Bollywood films _____ ।

Present Indefinite Tense - Negative Sentence

In this section you will learn the "negative form" of the present indefinite tense. You will use "nahī̃" नहीं to convey the negative form.

Case 1: Using the negative form when there is no action verb

- I am not a student.
- Maĩ student nahī̃ hū̃.
- मैं student नहीं हूँ ।

- You are not a student.
- Āp student nahī̃ haĩ.
- आप student नहीं हैं ।

- They are not students.
- Ve students nahī̃ haĩ.
- वे students नहीं हैं ।

- We are not students.
- Hum students nahī̃ haĩ.
- हम students नहीं हैं ।

- He is not a student.
- Vah student nahī̃ hai.
- वह student नहीं है ।

Go ahead and complete the following challenges.

Exercise 5.3 Help Pingu convert the following sentences into negative form.

1. Vah American hai.   १ वह American है ।
2. Hum protesters haĩ.   २ हम protesters हैं ।
3. Vah lambā hai.   ३ वह लंबा है ।
4. Hum pareshān haĩ.   ४ हम परेशान हैं ।
5. Vah funny hai.   ५ वह funny है ।

Case 2: Using the negative form when there is an action verb.

The concept remains the same. You will use "nahī̃" before the action verb.

- I do not walk. *(male)*
- Maī̃ nahī̃ chaltā hū̃. *(male)*
- मैं नहीं चलता हूँ ।

- I do not walk. *(female)*
- Maī̃ nahī̃ chaltī hū̃. *(female)*
- मैं नहीं चलती हूँ ।

- You do not walk.
- Āp nahī̃ chalte haī̃.
- आप नहीं चलते हैं ।

- We do not walk.
- Hum nahī̃ chalte haī̃.
- हम नहीं चलते हैं ।

- They do not walk.
- Ve nahī̃ chalte haī̃.
- वे नहीं चलते हैं ।

- He does not walk.
- Vah nahī̃ chaltā hai.
- वह नहीं चलता है ।

- She does not walk.
- Vah nahī̃ chaltī hai.
- वह नहीं चलती है ।

Exercise 5.4 Help Pingu translate the following sentences in Hindi.

1. I do not play cricket in India.
2. They do not drink chai in the morning.
3. We do not speak french.
4. You do not sleep on time.
5. He does not sing bhajan everyday.
6. She does not watch Bollywood movies.

Present Indefinite Tense - Interrogative Sentence

Interrogatives are sentences where you are asking questions. See examples below:

- Are you sick?
- Is she coming to school?

To form Hindi interrogative sentences, you will put "kyā" (क्या) at the beginning of the sentence. Such sentences are also known as yes-no questions, since the expected answer is either yes or no.

Case 1: Using the interrogative form when there is no action verb

- Am I a student?
  - Kyā maĩ student hũ?
  - क्या में student हूँ ?

- Are you a student?
  - Kyā āp student haĩ?
  - क्या आप student हैं ?

- Are they students?
  - Kyā ve students haĩ?
  - क्या वे students हैं ?

- Are we students?
  - Kyā hum students haĩ?
  - क्या हम students हैं ?

- Is he a student?
  - Kyā vah student hai?
  - क्या वह student है ?

Exercise 5.5 Help Pingu guess Prakash's question based on Rita's response.

Prakash: _____? *Rita*: Jī nahĩ, vah American nahĩ hai, Indian hai.

Prakash: _____? *Rita*: Jī hā̃, hum lambe haĩ.

Prakash: _____? *Rita*: Jī hā̃, vah ek mathematician hai.

Prakash: _____? *Rita*: Jī hā̃, tum bahut lucky ho.

Prakash: _____? *Rita*: Nahĩ, vah funny nahĩ hai.

Case 2: Using the interrogative form, when there is an action verb.

- Do I walk? *(male)*
- Kyā maĩ chaltā hū̃? *(male)*
- क्या मैं चलता हूँ ?

- Do I walk? *(male)*
- Kyā maĩ chaltī hū̃? *(female)*
- क्या मैं चलती हूँ ?

- Do you walk?
- Kyā āp chalte haĩ?
- क्या आप चलते हैं ?

- Do we walk?
- Kyā hum chalte haĩ?
- क्या हम चलते हैं ?

- Do they walk?
- Kyā ve chalte haĩ?
- क्या वे चलते हैं ?

- Does he walk?
- Kyā vah chaltā hai?
- क्या वह चलता है ?

- Does she walk?
- Kyā vah chaltī hai?
- क्या वह चलती है ?

Exercise 5.6 Help Pingu transform the following sentences into the interrogative.

1. Ve India mẽ cricket khelte haĩ.
2. Āp subah chāy pīte haĩ.
3. Vah French boltā hai.
4. Āp samay pe sote haĩ.
5. Vah roz bhajan gātī hai.
6. Āp Bollywood movies dekhte haĩ.

१ वे India में cricket खेलते हैं ।
२ आप सुबह चाय पीते हैं ।
३ वह French बोलता है ।
४ आप समय पे सोते हैं ।
५ वह रोज़ भजन गाती है ।
६ आप Bollywood movies देखते हैं ।

Present Indefinite Tense - Interrogative Negative Sentence

To combine the interrogative and negative scenarios, you will use "kyā" क्या at the beginning of the negative sentence that we learned above.

Case 1: Using the interrogative-negative form, when there is no action verb

- Am I not a student?
  - Kyā maĩ student nahī̃ hū̃?
  - क्या मैं student नहीं हूँ ?

- Are you not a student?
  - Kyā āp student nahī̃ haĩ?
  - क्या आप student नहीं हैं ?

- Are they not students?
  - Kyā ve students nahī̃ haĩ?
  - क्या वे students नहीं हैं ?

- Are we not students?
  - Kyā hum students nahī̃ haĩ?
  - क्या हम students नहीं हैं ?

- Is he not a student?
  - Kyā vah student nahī̃ hai?
  - क्या वह student नहीं है ?

Exercise 5.7 Help Pingu arrange the following words in the correct order to make a negative interrogative sentence.

1 nahī̃ - kyā - vah - hai - American - ?
2 lambe - nahī̃ - kyā - haĩ - hum - ?
3 hai - nurs - vah - kyā - nahī̃ - ?
4 kyā - hū̃ - maĩ - nahī̃ - lucky - ?
5 vah - nahī̃ - kyā - hai - funny - ?

१ नहीं - क्या - वह - है - American - ?
२ लंबे - नहीं - क्या - हैं - हम - ?
३ है - नर्स - वह - क्या - नहीं - ?
४ क्या - हूँ - मैं - नहीं - lucky - ?
५ वह - नहीं - क्या - है - funny - ?

Case 2: Using the negative interrogative form when there is an action verb.

The concept remains the same. You will use "kyā" at the beginning of the negative sentence we learned above.

- Do I not walk? *(male)*
- Kyā maĩ chaltā nahī̃ hū̃? *(male)*
- क्या मैं चलता नहीं हूँ ?

- Do I not walk? *(female)*
- Kyā maĩ chaltī nahī̃ hū̃? *(female)*
- क्या मैं चलती नहीं हूँ ?

- Do you not walk?
- Kyā āp chalte nahī̃ haĩ?
- क्या आप चलते नहीं हैं ?

- Do we not walk?
- Kyā hum chalte nahī̃ haĩ?
- क्या हम चलते नहीं हैं ?

- Do they not walk?
- Kyā ve chalte nahī̃ haĩ?
- क्या वे चलते नहीं हैं ?

- Does he not walk?
- Kyā vah chaltā nahī̃ hai?
- क्या वह चलता नहीं है ?

- Does she not walk?
- Kyā vah chaltī nahī̃ hai?
- क्या वह चलती नहीं है ?

Exercise 5.8 Help Pingu translate the following sentences into Hindi.

1. Don't they play cricket in India?
2. Do you not drink tea in the morning?
3. Doesn't he speak French?
4. Do you not sleep on time?
5. Doesn't she sing bhajan every day?

Your goal after completing chapter 5 is to talk about your daily routine in Hindi. See some of the writings from HindiUniversity students and get inspired.

> Watch the video "Asking time " at YouTube.com/HindiUniversity (playlist: Pingu Learns To Speak Hindi) to deepen your learning.

Get inspired by HindiUniversity students

Ashutosh (Washington DC)

Maī sat baje uthtā hū̃. Phir āth baje tak taiyār hotā hū̃. Maī roz ādhe ghante commute kartā hū̃. Maī nau baje office jātā hū̃. Maī nau baje se sādhe pā̃ch baje tak kām kartā hū̃. Shām ko maī apne bacchõ ke sāth kheltā hū̃. Sādhe āth baje me parents se bāt kartā hū̃.

मैं सात बजे उठता हूँ । फिर आठ बजे तक तैयार होता हूँ । मैं रोज़ आधे घंटे commute करता हूँ । मैं नौ बजे office जाता हूँ । मैं नौ बजे से साढ़े पाँच बजे तक काम करता हूँ । शाम को मैं अपने बच्चों के साथ खेलता हूँ । साढ़े साढ़े आठ बजे में parents से बात करता हूँ ।

Alessia (Italy)

Maī subah sāt baje uthtī hū̃. Phir sādhe āth baje tak taiyār hotī hū̃. Maī nau baje se sāt baje tak kām kartī hū̃. Maī sādhe bārah baje se tīn baje tak ārām kartī hū̃.

मैं सुबह सात बजे उठती हूँ । फिर साढ़े आठ बजे तक तैयार होती हूँ । मैं नौ बजे से सात बजे तक काम करती हूँ । मैं साढ़े बारह बजे से तीन बजे तक आराम करती हूँ ।

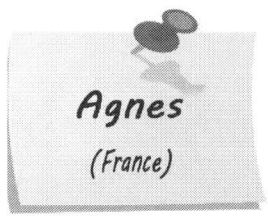

Agnes (France)

Maī roz savā chah baje jāgtī hū̃. Nahākar, maī sāt baje mere bacchõ ko school bhejtī hū̃. Phir, ghar pe breakfast banākar apne chote bete ko taiyār kartī hū̃. Maī āth baje usko school chodtī hū̃. Maī nau baje se das baje tak gym jātī hū̃. chār baje se pā̃ch baje ke beech maī mere bacchõ ko pick up kartī hū̃. Snacks khākar hum gruh kārya karte haī. Shām ko sāt baje, maī mere parivār ke liye khānā banātī hū̃. Aur āth baje hum sāth-sāth dinner khāte hai.

मैं रोज़ सवा छह बजे जागती हूँ । नहाकर , मैं अपने बच्चों को सुबह सात बजे स्कूल भेजती हूँ । फिर, घर पे breakfast बनाकर अपने छोटे बेटे को तैयार करती हूँ । मैं आठ बजे उसको स्कूल छोड़ती हूँ । मैं नौ बजे से दस बजे तक gym जाती हूँ । चार बजे से पाँच बजे के beech मैं मेरे बच्चों को pick up करती हूँ । Snacks खाकर हम गृहकार्य करते हैं । शाम को सात बजे, मैं मेरे परिवार के लिए खाना बनाती हूँ । और आठ बजे हम साथ साथ dinner खाते हैं ।

Chapter 6

What is Pingu doing right now?

+ Pingu will learn to talk about events in her life right now and form sentences in the present continuous tense.

Present Continuous Tense

In this chapter, my goal is to provide you with the tools to discuss things you are currently doing (i.e., at this moment). Such sentences are often expressed in the present continuous tense. See the examples below:

- I am eating right now.
- I am watching TV.

You will notice that these verbs end with "ing" (i.e., eating, watching, etc.). Irrespective of the pronoun (I, we, they, you, he, she), they all end with "ing".

```
                      present
                     continuous
past                    now                    future
```

In Hindi, the following are the rules for the verb conjugation:

Subject	Verb Conjugation (Chalnā)	Rules
Maĩ	Chal rahā *(male)* hũ. Chal rahī *(female)* hũ.	We use the base stem of the verb (i.e., chal), and along with that, we use "rahā" for masculine pronouns and "rahī" for feminine pronouns.
Tum	Chal rahe *(male)* ho. Chal rahī *(female)* ho.	We use the base stem of the verb (i.e., chal), and along with that, we use "rahe" for masculine pronouns and "rahī" for feminine pronouns.
Tū Vah / Yah	Chal rahā *(male)* hai. Chal rahī *(female)* hai.	We use the base stem of the verb (i.e., chal), and along with that, we use "rahā" for masculine pronouns and "rahī" for feminine pronouns.

Hum	Chal rahe *(male)* haĩ.	We use the base stem of the verb (i.e., chal), and along with that, we use "rahe" for masculine pronouns and "rahī" for feminine pronouns.
Āp	Chal rahī *(female)* haĩ.	
Ve / Ye		

"Chalnā" is our base verb, which means "to walk". In the scenarios above, we use the base stem of the verb "chal". Along with "chal", we use "rahā", "rahī" or "rahe" based on the pronoun (in this case, "chal" is also referred to as the <u>base stem</u>).

So our sentences will look like this:

- I am walking. *(male)*
  - Maĩ chal rahā hū̃. *(male)*
  - मैं चल रहा हूँ ।

- I am walking. *(female)*
  - Maĩ chal rahī hū̃. *(female)*
  - मैं चल रही हूँ ।

- You (familiar) are walking.
  - Tum chal rahe ho. *(male)*
  - तुम चल रहे हो ।

- You (intimate) are walking.
  - Tū chal rahā hai. *(male)*
  - तू चल रहा है ।

- He is walking.
  - Vah chal rahā hai.
  - वह चल रहा है ।

- She is walking.
  - Vah chal rahī hai.
  - वह चल रही है ।

- We are walking.
  - Hum chal rahe haĩ.
  - हम चल रहे हैं ।

- You are walking.
  - Āp chal rahe haĩ.
  - आप चल रहे हैं ।

- They are walking.
  - Ve chal rahe haĩ.
  - वे चल रहे हैं ।

Exercise 6.1 Help Pingu complete the following sentences with the correct present continuous form. (verb: dekhnā देखना = to watch)

1   Maĩ Hindī movie _____ . *(male)*   १   मैं हिन्दी movie _____ ।

2   Maĩ Hindī movie _____ . *(female)*   २   मैं हिन्दी movie _____ ।

3   Āp Hindī movie _____ .   ३   आप हिन्दी movie _____ ।

4   Hum Hindī movie _____ .   ४   हम हिन्दी movie _____ ।

5   Ve Hindī movie _____ .   ५   वे हिन्दी movie _____ ।

6   Vah Hindī movie _____ . *(he)*   ६   वह हिन्दी movie _____ ।

7   Vah Hindī movie _____ . *(she)*   ७   वह हिन्दी movie _____ ।

Exercise 6.2 Help Pingu translate the following sentences into Hindi (negative).

1   I am not giving a speech in school.
2   They are not eating food in the restaurant.
3   We are not learning Hindi.
4   You are not going to the office.
5   He is not singing bhajans in the temple.
6   She is not cleaning the house.
7   You are not sleeping.

Exercise 6.3 Help Pingu make present continuous sentences using the verbs below.

1. nāchnā नाचना	2. Sonā सोना	3. Ronā रोना
4. Sunnā सुनना	5. Hāsnā हँसना	6. Dhonā धोना

1 Āp _____ .
2 Vah _____ .
3 Tum _____ .
4 Hum music _____ .
5 Ve _____ .
6 Maĩ bartan _____ .

१ आप _____ ।
२ वह _____ ।
३ तुम _____ ।
४ हम music _____ ।
५ वे _____ ।
६ मैं बर्तन _____ ।

Exercise 6.4 Help Pingu translate the following sentences into Hindi.

1 Am I giving a speech in school?
2 Are they eating food in the restaurant?
3 Are we learning Hindi?
4 Are you going to the office?
5 Is he not singing bhajans in the temple?
6 Is she not cleaning the house?

Watch the video "Present Continuous Tense" at YouTube.com/HindiUniversity (playlist: Pingu Learns To Speak Hindi) to deepen your learning.

Hindi Vocabulary

English	Hindi	Devanagari
Weather	Mausam	मौसम
Village	Gã̄v	गाँव
Town	Kasbā	कस्बा
City	Shehar	शहर
Capital	Rājdhānī	राजधानी
Country	Desh	देश
Street	Galī	गली
Flower	Phūl	फूल
Victory	Jīt	जीत
Defeat	Hār	हार
To break	Toḍnā	तोड़ना
To lose	Hārnā	हारना
To win	Jītnā	जीतना
To sing	Gānā	गाना
To give up	Choḍnā	छोड़ना

Get inspired by HindiUniversity students

Your goal after completing Chapter 6 is to talk about things you are doing right now. See some of the writings from HindiUniversity students and get inspired.

Ashutosh (Washington DC)

Maĩ Hindi sikhā rahā hū̃. Maĩ aur mere dost ek Hindī kī kitāb likh rahe haĩ. Maĩ apne bacchõ ke sāth ghūm rahā hū̃. Maĩ apnā ghar thīk karwā rahā hū̃. Maĩ apnā wazan kam karne kī koshish kar rahā hū̃. Par merā wazan kam nahī̃ ho rahā hai. Maĩ apne parivār ke sāth achchhā samay bītā rahā hū̃. Maĩ talā huā khānā kam karne kī koshish kar rahā hū̃.

मैं हिन्दी सिखा रहा हूँ । मैं और मेरे दोस्त एक हिन्दी की किताब लिख रहे हैं । मैं अपने बच्चों के साथ घूम रहा हूँ । मैं अपना घर ठीक करवा रहा हूँ । मैं अपना वज़न कम करने की कोशिश कर रहा हूँ । पर मेरा वज़न कम नहीं हो रहा है । मैं अपने परिवार के साथ अच्छा समय बीता रहा हूँ । मैं तला हुआ खाना कम करने की कोशिश कर रहा हूँ ।

Liz (Colorado)

Maĩ WhatsApp par message likh rahī hū̃. Maĩ aur mere betā, Kyle ko Rocky Mountains dikhā rahe hai. Kyle merī French dost kā betā hai. Maĩ bacchõ ke sāth ghode par ride kar rahī hū̃.

मैं WhatsApp पर message लिख रही हूँ । मैं और मेरे बेटा, Kyle को Rocky Mountains दिखा रहे हैं । Kyle मेरी French दोस्त का बेटा है । मैं बच्चों के साथ घोड़े पर ride कर रही हूँ ।

Jenny (Germany)

Maĩ apne mātā pitā ke sāth Berlin jā rahī hū̃. Āj kā mausam bahut garam hai. Lekin bus ke andar air conditioner hai. Mere mātā pitā so rahe haĩ. Aur maĩ merī email check kar rahī hū̃. Mujhe lagtā hai ki hum dopahar tīn baje Berlin pahũchẽge.

मैं अपने माता-पिता के साथ Berlin जा रही हूँ । आज का मौसम बहुत गर्म है । लेकिन बस के अंदर air conditioner है । मेरे माता-पिता सो रहे हैं । और मैं मेरी email check कर रही हूँ । मुझे लगता कि हम दोपहर तीन बजे Berlin पहुँचेंगे ।

Chapter 7

Pingu's future plans

+ Pingu will learn to talk about her future plans in Hindi by forming sentences in the future indefinite tense.

Future Indefinite Tense

In this chapter, my goal is to provide you with the tools to discuss things/your future plans in Hindi. Such sentences are often expressed in the future indefinite tense. Examples include:

- I will watch the "Harry Potter" series next month.
- I will perform at the concert tomorrow.

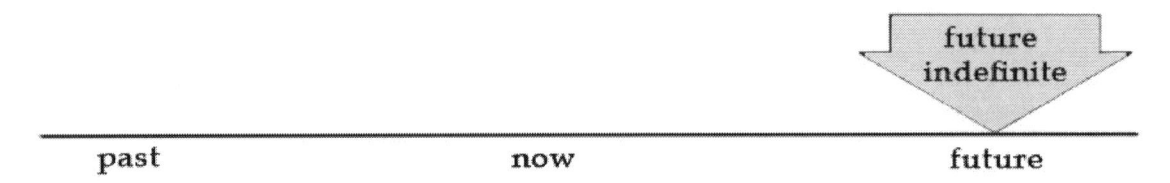

Note that when forming English sentences in the future tense, the verbs are preceded by "will" (i.e., will eat, will cook, will watch, etc.), irrespective of the pronouns (I, we, they, you, he, she) used. However, in Hindi, the verb conjugation varies based on the pronoun used.

Following are the rules for the verb conjugation in Hindi:

Subject	Verb (Chalnā)	Rules
Maĩ	Chalū̃gā. *(male)* Chalū̃gī. *(female)*	Replace "nā" in the verb with "ū̃gā" for masculine pronouns, and "ū̃gī" for feminine pronouns.
Tum	Chaloge. *(male)* Chalogī. *(female)*	Replace "nā" in the verb with "oge" for masculine pronouns, and "ogī" for feminine pronouns.
Tū	Chalegā. *(male)* Chalegī. *(female)*	Replace "nā" in the verb with "egā" for masculine pronouns, and "egī" for feminine pronouns.
Vah / Yah		
Āp	Chalẽge. *(male)* Chalẽgī. *(female)*	Replace "nā" in the verb with "ẽge" for masculine pronouns, and "ẽgī" for feminine pronouns.
Hum		
Ye / Ve		

Based on the rules above, our sentences will look like this:

- I will walk. *(male)*
- I will walk. *(female)*
- You (familiar) will walk. *(male)*
- He will walk.
- She will walk.
- We will walk.
- You will walk.
- They will walk.

- Maĩ chalū̃gā.
- मैं चलूँगा ।
- Maĩ chalū̃gī.
- मैं चलूँगी ।
- Tum chaloge.
- तुम चलोगे ।
- Vah chalegā.
- वह चलेगा ।
- Vah chalegī.
- वह चलेगी ।
- Hum chalẽge.
- हम चलेंगे |
- Āp chalẽge.
- आप चलेंगे ।
- Ve chalẽge.
- वे चलेंगे ।

Exercise 7.1 Help Pingu make future indefinite sentences using the verbs below.

| jānā | sīkhnā | sāf karnā | denā | gānā | khānā |

1 Vah ghar _____ .
2 Hum Hindī _____ .
3 Āp daftar ko _____ .
4 Maĩ skūl mẽ speech _____ .
5 Vah temple mẽ bhajan _____ .
6 Ve restaurant mẽ khānā _____ .

१ वह घर _____ ।
२ हम हिन्दी _____ ।
३ आप दफ़्तर को _____ ।
४ मैं स्कूल में speech _____ ।
५ वह temple में भजन _____ ।
६ वे restaurant में खाना _____ ।

Exercise 7.2 Help Pingu write sentences in the future indefinite using the verbs below.

1. Uthnā उठना	2. Sīkhnā सीखना	3. Pīnā पीना
4. Sāf karnā साफ़ करना	5. Jānā जाना	6. Likhnā लिखना

1 Viju _____ .
2 Ve _____ .
3 Sarah chāy _____ .
4 Hum ghar _____ .
5 Bacche school _____ .
6 Maĩ ek patr *(male)* _____ .

१ Viju _____ ।
२ वे _____ ।
३ Sarah चाय _____ ।
४ हम घर _____ ।
५ बच्चे school _____ ।
६ मैं एक पत्र _____ ।

Exercise 7.3 Help Pingu translate the following sentences into Hindi (negative). Please refer to earlier chapters if you do not know the Hindi verbs.

1 I will not give a speech at school.
2 They won't eat food in the restaurant.
3 We won't learn Hindi.
4 You won't speak there tomorrow.
5 He won't ask me.
6 She won't respond.

Exercise 7.4 Help Pingu translate the following sentences into Hindi (interrogative). Please refer to earlier chapters if you do not know the Hindi verbs.

1. Will you give a speech at school?
2. Will they eat seafood?
3. Will they travel to Costa Rica?
4. Will they meet the president?
5. Will she perform at the ceremony tomorrow?
6. Will she clean the house?

Exercise 7.5 Help Pingu translate the following sentences into Hindi (negative + interrogative). Refer to the earlier chapters if you do not know the Hindi verbs.

1. Won't you give a speech at school tomorrow?
2. Won't they forget?
3. Won't we go home?
4. Won't you stay in Italy?
5. Won't I look nice?
6. Won't he clean the house?

Watch the video "Future Indefinite Tense" at YouTube.com/HindiUniversity (playlist: Pingu Learns To Speak Hindi) to deepen your learning.

Hindi Vocabulary

English	Hindi	Devanagari
Today / Tomorrow	Kal	कल
Monday	Somvār	सोमवार
Tuesday	Māgalvār	मंगलवार
Wednesday	Budhvār	बुधवार
Thursday	Guruvār	गुरुवार
Friday	Shukravār	शुक्रवार
Saturday	Shanivār	शनिवार
Sunday	Ravivār	रविवार
Next day	Agle din	अगले दिन
Next week	Agle saptāh	अगले सप्ताह
Next month	Agle mahīne	अगले महीने
Maybe	Shāyad	शायद
To ask	Pūchhnā	पूछना
To answer	Javāb denā	जवाब देना
To look, to appear	Dikhnā	दिखना
To forget	Bhūlnā	भूलना
To remember	Yād karnā	याद करना

Get inspired by HindiUniversity students

Your goal after completing this chapter is to talk about your future plans in Hindi. See some of the writings from HindiUniversity students and get inspired.

Chelsea (USA)

Maĩ agle hafte apne dostõ ke sāth Denver jāũgī. Vahā̃ hum kām karẽge aur hum maze bhī karẽge. Shāyad, maĩ apnī dost, Liz se milũ̄gī. Maĩ Denver mẽ Estes Park jāũgī. Maĩ pahādõ ko dekhũgī.

मैं अगले हफ्ते अपने दोस्तों के साथ Denver जाऊँगी । वहाँ हम काम करेंगे और हम मज़े भी करेंगे। शायद , मैं अपनी दोस्त , Liz से मिलूँगी । मैं Denver में Estes Park जाऊँगी । मैं पहाड़ों को देखूँगी ।

Rea (Taiwan)

Maĩ 4th bār India ghūmne jā rahī hū̃. Yah yātrā bahut special hai kyõ ki maĩ apne students ke sāth jāũgī. Yah unkī pehlī India kī yātrā hai. Hum Delhi, Jaipur aur Agra jāẽge. Hum purāne qile (fort) dekhẽge. Hum apne Indian dostõ se milẽge aur sāth mẽ dinner khāẽge. Hum India jāne ke liye taiyār haĩ. INDIA phir milẽge.

मैं चौथी बार India घूमने जा रही हूँ । यह यात्रा बहुत special है क्योंकि मैं अपने students के साथ जाऊँगी । यह उनकी पहली India की यात्रा है । हम दिल्ली, जयपुर और आगरा जाएँगे । हम पुराने किले देखेंगे । हम अपने Indian दोस्तों से मिलेंगे और साथ में diner खाएँगे । हम India जाने के लिए तैयार हैं । INDIA फिर मिलेंगे ।

Agnes (France)

Maĩ agle sāl, merī betī ke liye school dhū̃dū̃gī. Maĩ apne parivār ke liye summer holidays plan karū̃gī. Maĩ agle mahīne apne bete ko English college mẽ bhejū̃gī. Merā sapnā hai ki maĩ pūrā Bhārat ghūmū̃. Maĩ dhārāpravāh Hindī bolnā chāhtī hū̃. Maĩ bhavishy mẽ Bhārat mẽ kām karnā chāhtī hū̃.

मैं अगले साल मेरी बेटी के लिए school ढूँढूँगी । मैं अपने परिवार के लिए summer holidays plan करुँगी । मैं अगले महीने अपने बेटे को English college में भेजूँगी । मेरा सपना है कि मैं पूरा भारत घूमूँ । मैं धारा प्रवाह हिन्दी बोलना चाहती हूँ । मैं भविष्य में भारत में काम करना चाहती हूँ ।

Chapter 8
Things Pingu used to do

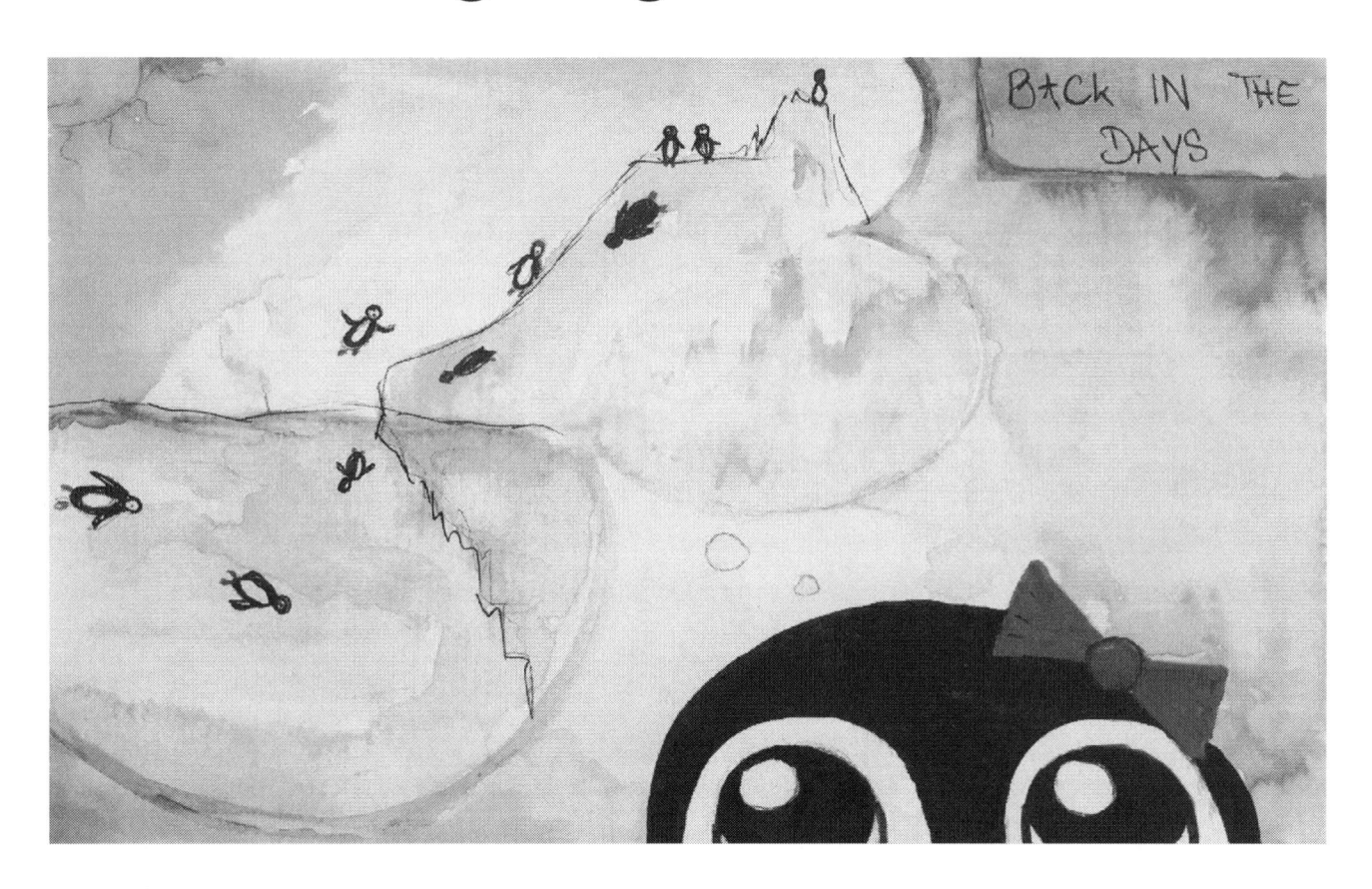

Pingu misses home and wants to reminisce. She will tell you all the things she used to do back home by forming sentences in the past indefinite tense.

Past Indefinite

In this chapter, my goal is to provide you with the tools to discuss things you used to do in the past in Hindi (i.e., things you used to do before COVID 19). You can form a wide variety of sentences in the past tense. Let's start with the simplest form first:

- I was _____
- You were _____
- He/She was _____
- We were _____
- You were _____
- They were _____

In the above sentences, the "to be" forms of the verbs are "was", "were". We have something similar in Hindi. If you recall from earlier chapters, when we formed sentences in the present tense (i.e., I am a student, you are a student), they often ended with "hū̃" and "ho" respectively. Here, we will use the past tense forms of "to be" (i.e., I was a student, you were a student). The table below shows the past tense form of "to be" for various pronouns.

English	Hindi	Devanagari
I was _____ . *(male) / (female)*	Maĩ _____ thā / thī .	मैं _____ था / थी ।
You were _____ . *(male) / (female)*	Tum _____ the / thī̃ .	तुम _____ थे / थीं ।
You were _____ . *(male) / (female)*	Tū _____ thā / thī .	तू _____ था / थी ।
He was _____ .	Vah/Yah _____ thā .	वह / यह _____ था ।
She was _____ .	Vah/Yah _____ thī .	वह / यह _____ थी ।
We were _____ . *(male) / (female)*	Hum _____ the / thī̃ .	हम _____ थे / थीं ।
You were _____ . *(male) / (female)*	Āp _____ the / thī̃ .	आप _____ थे / थीं ।
They were _____ . *(male) / (female)*	Ve/Ye _____ the / thī̃ .	वे / ये _____ थे / थीं ।

Let's add some objects in these constructs and have fun making simple Hindi sentences in the past tense.

Case 1: Using the past forms of "to be"

- I was a student. *(male)*
- Maĩ student thā. *(male)*
- मैं student था ।

- You were a student.
- Āp student the.
- आप student थे ।

- They were students.
- Ve students the.
- वे students थे ।

- We were students.
- Hum students the.
- हम students थे ।

- She was a student.
- Vah student thī.
- वह student थी ।

I encourage you to go over the cases described in Chapter 1 and try saying them in the past form, as shown above.

> Watch the video "Past Indefinite Tense" at YouTube.com/HindiUniversity (playlist: Pingu Learns To Speak Hindi) to deepen your learning.

Case 2: Using the "action verbs"

We all have memories we want to talk about including our childhood activities, old habits, old friends, etc. Examples include:

- I used to watch "Harry Potter".
- I used to perform on stage.

You will notice that in English, these verbs are preceded by "used to" (i.e., used to eat, used to cook, used to watch,etc.), irrespective of the pronouns (I, we, they, you, he, she).

In Hindi, the rules for the verb conjugation are listed in the table ahead:

Subject	Verb conjugation (chalnā)	Rules
Maĩ	Chaltā *(Male)* thā. Chaltī *(Female)* thī.	Replace the "nā" in the verb with "tā". Replace the "nā" in the verb with "tī".
Tum	Chalte *(Male)* the. Chaltī *(Female)* thĩ.	Replace the "nā" in the verb with "te" Replace the "nā" in the verb with "tī".
Tū	Chaltā *(Male)* thā. Chaltī *(Female)* thī	Replace the "nā" in the verb with "tā". Replace the "nā" in the verb with "tī".
Vah / Yah		
Hum	Chalte *(Male)* the. Chaltī *(Female)* thĩ.	Replace the "nā" in the verb with "te". Replace the "nā" in the verb with "tī".
Āp		
Ve / Ye		

"Chalnā" is our base verb, which means "to walk". In the scenarios above, we have replaced "nā" with "tā", "tī" or "te" based on the pronoun.

So our sentences will look like this:

- I used to walk. *(male)*
  - Maĩ chaltā thā. *(male)*
  - मैं चलता था ।

- I used to walk. *(female)*
  - Maĩ chaltī thī. *(female)*
  - मैं चलती थी ।

- You (familiar) used to walk.
  - Tum chalte the. *(male)*
  - तुम चलते थे ।

- He used to walk.
  - Vah chaltā thā.
  - वह चलता था ।

- She used to walk.
  - Vah chaltī thī.
  - वह चलती थी ।

- We used to walk.
  - Hum chalte the.
  - हम चलते थे ।

- You used to walk.
- Āp chalte the.
- आप चलते थे ।

- They used to walk.
- Ve chalte the.
- वे चलते थे ।

Exercise 8.1 Help Pingu complete the following sentences with the right verb conjugation (verb: dekhnā देखना = to watch).

1. Maĩ Hindī movie _____ . *(male)*
2. Maĩ Hindī movie _____ . *(female)*
3. Āp Hindī movie _____ .
4. Hum Hindī movie _____ .
5. Ve Hindī movie _____ .
6. Vah Hindī movie _____ . *(he)*
7. Vah Hindī movie _____ . *(she)*

१ मैं हिन्दी movie _____ ।
२ मैं हिन्दी movie _____ ।
३ आप हिन्दी movie _____ ।
४ हम हिन्दी movie _____ ।
५ वे हिन्दी movie _____ ।
६ वह हिन्दी movie _____ ।
७ वह हिन्दी movie _____ ।

Exercise 8.2 Help Pingu choose the correct verb and put it in the proper past form.

| jānā | sīkhnā | karnā | denā | gānā | khānā |

1. Maĩ skūl mẽ bhāshan _____ .
2. Vah ghar sāf _____ .
3. Ham bhāshā _____ .
4. Āp USPS mẽ kām _____ .
5. Vah temple mẽ bhajan _____ .
6. Ve restaurant mẽ thai khānā _____ .

१ मैं स्कूल में भाषण _____ ।
२ वह घर साफ़ _____ ।
३ हम भाषा _____ ।
४ आप USPS में काम _____ ।
५ वह temple में भजन _____ ।
६ वे restaurant में thai खाना _____ ।

Exercise 8.3 Now, help Pingu complete the sentences from Exercise 8.2 in the past negative form.

Exercise 8.4 Help Pingu arrange the following words in the correct order.

1 pitā - kyā - thā - vah ?
2 kyā - thī - cīzẽ - vah - bhūltī - ?
3 hum - yahā̃ - the - kyā - khelte ?
4 the - party - mẽ - merī - āp - āte - kyā ?
5 acchā - dikhtā - maĩ - kyā - thā ?
6 complain - ve - the - kyā - karte - ?

१ पीता - क्या - था - वह ?
२ क्या - थी - चीज़ें - वह - भूलती ?
३ हम - यहाँ - थे - क्या - खेलते ?
४ थे - party - में - मेरी - आप - आते - क्या ?
५ अच्छा - दिखता - मैं - क्या - था ?
६ complain - वे - थे - क्या - करते - ?

Exercise 8.5 Help Pingu correct the following paragraph.

Merā nām Alessia hai. Chah baje uthtī hai. Phir, maĩ sādhe sāt baje tak taiyār honā thī. Maĩ sādhe sāt baje se pā̃ch baje tak babysit kartī thā. Aur weekends maĩ navy drill pe jātā thī. Bād mẽ chār baje se pā̃ch baje tak, maĩ dinner banāte thī. Phir, maĩ ghar kā kām kartī thā.

मेरा नाम Alessia है । छह बजे उठती है । फिर, मैं साढ़े सात बजे तक तैयार होना थी । मैं साढ़े सात बजे से पाँच बजे तक babysit करती था । और weekends पे navy drill पे जाता थी । बाद में चार बजे से पाँच बजे तक , मैं dinner बनाते थी । फिर , मैं घर का काम करती था ।

Hindi Vocabulary

English	Hindi	Devanagari
Weekend	Saptāhā̃t	सप्ताहांत
Hour	Ghantā	घंटा
Day	Din	दिन
Week	Saptāh	सप्ताह
Month	Mahīnā	महीना
Year	Sāl	साल
Morning	Subah	सुबह
Noon	Dopahar	दोपहर
Evening	Shām	शाम
Night	Rāt	रात
To prepare	Taiyār karnā	तैयार करना
To clean	Sāf karnā	साफ करना
To work	Kām karnā	काम करना

Before you start with the next section, I recommend you watch this short video.

Watch the video "Asking time " at YouTube.com/HindiUniversity (playlist: Pingu Learns To Speak Hindi) to deepen your learning.

Get inspired by HindiUniversity students

Your goal, after completing this chapter, is to talk about things you used to do in your childhood. See some of the writings from HindiUniversity students and get inspired.

Alessia (Italy)

Maī subah sādhe sāt baje uthtī thī. Phir sādhe āth baje tak taiyār hotī thī. Maī nau baje se sāt baje tak kām kartī thī. Maī sādhe bārah baje se tīn baje tak ārām kartī thī. Shām ko maī do ghante gym jātī thī. Maī calligraphy aur handwriting bahut pasand kartī thī.

मैं सुबह साढ़े सात बजे उठती थी । फिर साढ़े आठ बजे तक तैयार होती थी । मैं नौ बजे से सात बजे तक काम करती थी । मैं साढ़े बारह बजे से तीन बजे तक आराम करती थी । शाम को मैं दो घंटे gym जाती थी । मैं calligraphy और handwriting बहुत पसंद करती थी ।

Rea (Taiwan)

Maī āth baje uthtī thī. Phir sādhe āth baje tak taiyār hotī thī aur scooter se office jātī thī. Maī nau baje se pāch baje tak office mē kām kartī thī. Phir shām ko sāt baje se āth baje tak bhāratiya dance sikhatī thī. Nau baje se bārah baje tak TV dekhtī thī aur ārām kartī thī.

मैं आठ बजे उठती थी । फिर साढ़े आठ बजे तक तैयार होती थी और scooter से office जाती थी । मैं नौ बजे से पाँच बजे तक office में काम करती थी । फिर शाम को सात बजे से आठ बजे तक भारतीय dance सिखाती थी । नौ बजे से बारह बजे तक TV देखती थी और आराम करती थी ।

Karolina (New Jersey)

Maī Chah baje uthtī thī. Phir, maī savā sāt baje se sādhe sāt baje tak taiyār hotī thī. Maī sādhe sāt baje se pāch baje tak babysit kartī thī. Bād mē pāch baje se chhah baje tak, maī dinner banātī thī. Phir, maī ghar kā kām kartī thī aur gyāra baje so jātī thī. Saptāhāt pe navy drill pe jātī thī

मैं छह बजे उठती थी । फिर, मैं सवा सात बजे से साढ़े सात बजे तक तैयार होती थी । मैं साढ़े सात बजे से पाँच बजे तक babysit करती थी । बाद में पाँच बजे से छह बजे तक , मैं dinner बनाती थी । फिर, मैं घर का काम करती थी और ग्यारह बजे सो जाती थी । सप्ताहांत पे navy drill पे जाती थी ।

Chapter 9
What did Pingu do?

+ Pingu will talk about her mistakes, the food she enjoyed, the places she traveled, and many more things in Hindi.

Past Tense

In this chapter, my goal is to provide you with the tools to discuss things you "did" in the past in Hindi. Such sentences are used when you are talking about the trip you made, the food you ate, the activities you did, etc.

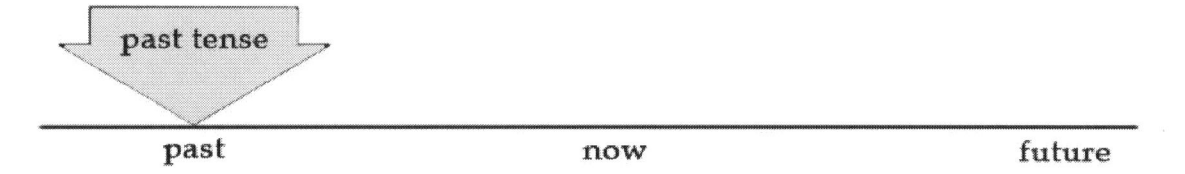

Transitive vs. Intransitive Verbs

You may be wondering why we are learning about transitive and intransitive verbs now. We have already covered so many tenses (present indefinite, present continuous, future indefinite, and past indefinite). The reason is, the Hindi language follows certain rules when forming sentences <u>in the past tense</u>. The verb conjugation depends on the type of verb (transitive or intransitive). Let's see some examples of both transitive and intransitive verbs are used in Hindi.

<u>Transitive Verbs</u>

- I ate an apple.
- We drank tea yesterday.
- They called the police.
- He called his mother.
- I wrote a book.
- She watched a movie.

<u>Intransitive Verbs</u>

- I went to India.
- We arrived today.
- They slept yesterday.
- He laughed.
- I cried.
- She sat under the tree.

Do you notice any difference between the transitive and intransitive sentences? Please don't give up and spend a few more minutes before moving on. If you notice carefully, the transitive verbs have "direct objects" that receive the verb's actions.

- She ate an apple.

In this case, "apple" is the direct object of the verb "eat". The verbs which always require an object to give them a meaning are called "transitive verbs". There is a trick to identify if the given verb is a transitive verb or not.

The trick: Convert the sentence to a question as shown below. If you get an answer, it is a "transitive verb".

- What did she eat?

The answer in this case is "apple". Thus, the verb "eat" is used as a transitive verb.

Let's look at another example:

- He called his mother.

Now, if you are still unsure if the verb "call" is transitive or intransitive, you will use the trick above and convert this into a question.

- Whom did he call?

The answer, in this case, is "mother". Thus, the verb "call" is a transitive verb as well.

In both of the scenarios above, "what" and "whom" help you determine that there is an object receiving the verb's action. However, if using "what" or "whom" doesn't make sense or doesn't give you an answer, this could mean that the verb is most likely an "intransitive verb".

Consider this example now: She sat under the tree.

If I translate the above using the trick, it will be:
- What did she sit? (X)
- Whom did she sit? (X)

Neither one of the questions above make sense. Thus, the verb in question (i.e., sit) is intransitive.

Our criterion for a "transitive verb" is that it should help you answer "What" or "Whom". Let's do some exercises to master this rule.

Exercise 9.1 Help Pingu classify the highlighted verbs as transitive or intransitive.

1. He came home.
2. I gave a speech in school.

3   They ate Thai food in the restaurant.
4   We walked together.
5   She spoke in French.
6   You went to Canada.

English	Hindi	Devanagari	T / I
To come	Ānā	आना	Intransitive
To give	Denā	देना	Transitive
To eat	Khānā	खाना	Transitive
To walk	Chalnā	चलना	Intransitive
To speak	Bolnā	बोलना	Intransitive
To go	Jānā	जाना	Intransitive

Since this exercise is a bit complicated, I will help out. Note how I have converted the above sentences into questions.

He came home.	What did he come? (X) Whom did he come? (X)	Intransitive
I gave a speech at school.	What did you give? (Y)	Transitive
They ate Thai food at the restaurant.	What did they eat? (Y)	Transitive.
We walked together.	What did we walk? (X) Whom did we walk? (X) How did we walk? (Y)	Intransitive.
She spoke politely.	What did she speak? (X) Whom did she speak? (X) How did she speak? (Y)	Intransitive.
You went to Canada.	What did you go? (X) Whom did you go? (X) Where did you go? (Y)	Intransitive

Using intransitive verbs in the past tense

In the previous chapter, we made Hindi sentences to convey things that we "used to" do. Examples include:

- I used to go to India.   Maĩ India jāta thā.
- They used to sleep at night.   Ve rāt ko sote the.

Sometimes, however, we convey events that have happened in the past using intransitive verbs. Some examples are provided below.

- They slept on time.
- He laughed.
- She walked.

The rules in Hindi for conjugating the intransitive verb chalnā (to walk) are:

Subject	Verb Conjugation (Chalnā)	Rules
Maĩ	Chalā *(Male)* Chalī *(Female)*	Replace "nā" in the verb with "ā". Replace "nā" in the verb with "ī".
Tum	Chale *(Male)* Chalī *(Female)*	Replace "nā" in the verb with "e". Replace "nā" in the verb with "ī".
Tū Vah / Yah	Chalā *(Male)* Chalī *(Female)*	Replace "nā" in the verb with "ā". Replace "nā" in the verb with "ī".
Hum Āp Ve / Ye	Chale *(Male)* Chalī *(Female)*	Replace "nā" in the verb with "e". Replace "nā" in the verb with "ī".

"Chalnā" is our base verb, which means "to walk". In the scenarios above, we have replaced "nā" with "ā", "ī" or "e" based on the pronoun.

So our sentences will look like this:

- I walked. *(male)*
  - Maĩ chalā. *(male)*
  - मैं चला ।

- I walked. *(female)*
  - Maĩ chalī. *(female)*
  - मैं चली ।

- You (familiar) walked.
  - Tum chale. *(male)*
  - तुम चले ।

- You (intimate) walked.
  - Tū chalā. *(male)*
  - तू चला ।

- He walked.
  - Vah chalā.
  - वह चला ।

- She walked.
  - Vah chalī.
  - वह चली ।

- We walked.
  - Hum chale.
  - हम चले ।

- You walked.
  - Āp chale.
  - आप चले ।

- They walked.
  - Ve chale.
  - वे चले ।

Exercise 9.2 Help Pingu complete the following sentences with the correct intransitive conjugation for the verb hãsnā (हँसना = to laugh) in the past tense.

1 Maĩ bahut _____ . *(male)*
2 Maĩ bahut _____ . *(female)*
3 Āp bahut _____ .
4 Hum bahut _____ .
5 Ve bahut _____ .
6 Vah bahut _____ . *(he)*
7 Vah bahut _____ . *(she)*

१ मैं बहुत _____ । *(male)*
२ मैं बहुत _____ । *(female)*
३ आप बहुत _____ ।
४ हम बहुत _____ ।
५ वे बहुत _____ ।
६ वह बहुत _____ । *(he)*
७ वह बहुत _____ । *(she)*

Exercise 9.3 Help Pingu translate the following sentences in Hindi (affirmative).

1. I laughed in school. *(male)*
2. They cried at the restaurant.
3. We spoke in French.
4. You swam in the pool.
5. They met at the temple.
6. She sat in the house.

Exercise 9.4 Help Pingu convert the sentences in Exercise 9.3 into the negative form.

Exercise 9.5 Help Pingu identify the error in each sentence and correct it.

1. Ve kal rāt ko jangal mẽ chaltā.	१ वे कल रात को जंगल में चलता ।
2. Vah samay pe uthe. *(he)*	२ वह समय पे उठे । *(he)*
3. Vah kal pool mẽ tairā. *(she)*	३ वह कल pool में तैरा । *(she)*
4. Hum bagīche mẽ kursiyõ pe baithe.	४ हम बगीचे में कुर्सियों पे बैठे ।
5. Kyā āp subah merī bahan se milnā?	५ क्या आप सुबह मेरी बहन से मिलना ?
6. Maĩ mere bete ke sāth Italian mẽ bole.	६ मैं मेरे बेटे के साथ Italian में बोले ।

Exercise 9.6 Help Pingu arrange the words in the correct order.

1. chale - ve - mẽ - nahī̃ - jangal	१ चले - वे - में - नहीं - जंगल
2. pe - kyā - samay - uthā - vah - nahī̃ ?	२ पे - क्या - समय - उठा - वह - नहीं ?
3. pool mẽ - kal - maĩ - tairā - nahī̃	३ pool में - कल - मैं - तैरा - नहीं
4. nahī̃ - mẽ - hum - bagīche - daude	४ नहीं - में - हम - बगीचे - दौड़े
5. kyā - nachī - party mẽ - vah ?	५ क्या - नाची - party में - वह ?
6. rehe - India mẽ - āp - kyā ?	६ रहे - India में - आप - क्या ?

Watch "Past Indefinite" & "Postposition NE" at YouTube.com/HindiUniversity (playlist: Pingu Learns To Speak Hindi) to deepen your learning.

Using transitive verbs in the past tense

In this section, we will focus on using transitive verbs in the past tense. Examples include the following:

- They ate Indian food.
- He narrated a story.
- I didn't say anything.

Before we move on, it's important to note that when transitive verbs are used in the past tense, we use a post-position called "Ne" after the nouns (i.e., Maĩ + Ne = Maĩne). See the table below to learn how the pronouns get modified when they are used with the postposition "ne".

Pronoun + ne		Outcome
Maĩ मैं	+ ne	Maĩne मैंने
Tum तुम		Tumne तुमने
Tū तू		Tūne तूने
Vah वह		Usne उसने
Yah यह		Isne इसने
Hum हम		Humne हमने
Āp आप		Āpne आपने
Ve वे		Unhõne उन्होंने
Ye ये		Inhõne इन्होंने

Now that we have learned the use of "ne", let's see how the transitive verbs get conjugated in the past tense.

Subject	Postposition (ne)	Object	Verb Conjugation (Likhnā)	Rules
Maĩ Tum Tū Āp Ve Hum Vah	ne	patr पत्र (letter) (singular masculine)	likhā लिखा	replace "nā" with "ā" for masc. singular object
		patr पत्र (letters) (plural masculine)	likhe लिखे	replace "nā" with "e" for masc. plural object
		kavitā कविता (poem) (singular feminine)	likhī लिखी	replace "nā" with "ī" for fem. singular object
		Kavitāẽ कविताएँ (poems) (plural feminine)	likhī̃ लिखीं	replace "nā" with "ī̃" for fem. plural object

Please note: The pronouns will be modified after adding postposition "ne", according to the previous table.

In the table above, "Likhnā" (to write) is the transitive verb. In the past indefinite tense, when you are using the transitive verbs, the verbs are conjugated based on the "objects" (i.e., patr, kavita, etc.), rather than the "subject" (i.e., Maĩ, Āp, Ve etc.). See the examples in the above table. Our sentences will look like this for the pronoun "maĩ":

- Maĩne patr likā. (I wrote a letter.) मैंने एक पत्र लिखा ।
- patr is considered "masculine singular".

- Maĩne patr likhe. (I wrote letters.) मैंने पत्र लिखे ।
- patr is considered "masculine plural". *Note that the plural of patr is patr.*

- Maĩne kavitā likhī. (I wrote a poem.) मैंने एक कविता लिखी ।
- kavitā is considered "feminine singular".

- Maĩne kavitāẽ likhī̃. (I wrote poems.) मैंने कविताएँ लिखीं ।
- kavitāẽ is considered "feminine plural".

Let's look at one more rule for transitive verbs. The base stem of some transitive verbs end with vowel sounds. For example "to eat" is khana in Hindi. If we remove "nā", it would be "kha", ending with a vowel sound "ā". For these types of verbs, we replace "nā" with "yā", "ye", "yī", "yī̃". See the table below.

Subject	Postposition (ne)	Object	Verb Conjugation (Khānā)	Rules
Maĩ Tum Tū Āp Ve Hum Vah	ne	seb सेब (apple) (masculine singular)	khāyā खाया	replace "nā" with "yā"
		samose समोसे (samosas) (masculine plural)	khāye खाये	replace "nā" with "ye"
		strawberry (feminine singular)	khāyī खायी	replace "nā" with "yī"
		jalebiyā̃ जलेबियाँ (feminine plural)	khāyī̃ खायीं	replace "nā" with "yī̃"

In the table above, our sentences will look like this for the pronoun "maĩ":

- Maĩne seb khāyā. (I ate an apple.)   मैंने सेब खाया ।
- Apple is considered "masculine singular".

- Maĩne samose khāye. (I ate samosas.)   मैंने समोसे खाये ।
- Samose is considered "masculine plural".

- Maĩne strawberry khāyī. (I ate a strawberry.)   मैंने strawberry खायी ।
- Strawberry is considered "feminine singular".

- Maĩne jalebiyā̃ khāyī̃. (I ate jalebis.)   मैंने जलेबियाँ खायीं ।
- Jalebiyā̃ is considered "feminine plural".

You may still have questions on how to decide which noun is masculine or feminine in Hindi. You are on the right track, and I highly encourage you to review chapter 2 and 3.

Exercise 9.7 Help Pingu complete the following sentences with the right verb conjugation (verb: banānā बनाना = to make).

1. Maĩne chāi _____ .
2. Maĩne samose _____ .
3. Āpne rotiyā̃ _____ .
4. Humne halwā _____ .
5. Unhõne lassī _____ .
6. Usne juice _____ .
7. Usne ice-cream _____ .

१ मैंने चाय _____ ।
२ मैंने समोसे _____ ।
३ आपने रोटियाँ _____ ।
४ हमने हलवा _____ ।
५ उन्होंने लस्सी _____ ।
६ उसने juice _____ ।
७ उसने ice-cream _____ ।

Hint:

- Chāi, Rotī, Lassī, Ice cream are feminine.
- Samosā, Halwā, Juice are masculine.

Exercise 9.8 Help Pingu translate the following sentences in Hindi.

1. I saw the movie.
2. She didn't eat the Margherita pizza.
3. You didn't buy the camera.
4. We listened to Bollywood songs.
5. He didn't sell the house.
6. They sang spiritual bhajans.
7. I didn't see the movie.
8. You bought the camera.

Exercise 9.9 Help Pingu translate the following sentences into Hindi.

1. Did you see the movie?
2. Did she eat the Margherita pizza?
3. Did we listen to Bollywood songs?
4. Didn't they sing spiritual bhajans?
5. Didn't you buy the camera?
6. Didn't he sell the house?

Hindi Vocabulary

English	Hindi	Devanagari
Potato	Ālū	आलू
Food	Khānā	खाना
Restaurant	Bhojnālay	भोजनालय
Temple	Mandir	मंदिर
Pool	Parnatāl	तरणताल
Garden	Bagīchā	बगीचा
Forest	Jangal	जंगल
Song	Gīt / Gānā	गीत / गाना
To bring	Lānā	लाना
To meet	Milnā	मिलना
To sell	Bechnā	बेचना
To sit	Baithnā	बैठना

Get inspired by HindiUniversity students

Tara (Iran)

Kal maĩ nāshtā karne ke bād bāzār gayī aur maīne sabjiyā̃ kharīdī. Phir maĩ ghar vāpas āyi. Maīne ghar sāf kiyā. Phir maīne apne dostõ ko phon kiyā aur unko apne ghar bulāyā. Ve bārah baje āye aur humne sāth mẽ lunch kiyā. Humne khāne ke bād bāt kī aur bahut hāse. Ve pā̃ch baje gaye. Maīne bartan dhoe, phir taiyār ho gayī aur parivār ke sāth park gayī. Humne vahā̃ ek ghante tak baidamītan khelā, phir hum ghar vāpas āye. Rāt ke khāne ke bād maīne TV dekhā aur kitāb padhī. Gyārah baje maīne light band kī aur maĩ soyī.

कल मैं नाश्ता करने के बाद बाज़ार गयी और मैंने सब्ज़ियाँ खरीदी । फिर मैं घर वापस आयी । मैंने घर साफ किया । फिर मैंने अपने दोस्तों को फोन किया और उनको अपने घर बुलाया । वे बारह बजे आये और हमने साथ में lunch किया । हमने खाने के बाद बात की और बहुत हँसे । वे पाँच बजे गये । मैंने बर्तन धोए , फिर तैयार हो गयी और परिवार के साथ park गयी । हमने वहाँ एक घंटे तक बैडमिंटन खेला , फिर हम घर वापस आये । रात के खाने के बाद मैंने TV देखा और किताब पढ़ी । ग्यारह बजे मैंने light बंद की और मैं सोयी ।

Rea (Taiwan)

Kal maīne apnī gādī thīk kī. Maīne apne tīsre bete ke sāth tennis khelā. Maīne apne bacchõ ke liye khānā banāyā. Maīne apne bagīce mẽ kām kiyā. Maīne apnā Hindī kā homework kiyā. Maĩ dance class mẽ gayī.

Pichhle saptāh, maīne apne students ko Bhangra sikhāyā. Maīne unke sāth perform kiyā. Maīne wazan kam karne kī koshish kī.

कल मैंने अपनी गाड़ी ठीक की । मैंने अपने तीसरे बेटे के साथ tennis खेला । मैंने अपने बच्चों के लिए sखाना बनाया । मैंने अपने बगीचे में काम किया । मैंने अपना हिन्दी का homework किया । मैं dance class में गयी ।
 पिछले सप्ताह , मैंने अपने students को Bhangra सिखाया । मैंने उनके साथ perform किया । मैंने वज़न कम करने की कोशिश की ।

Chapter 10

What can Pingu do?

+ You may wonder what Pingu can do besides learning Hindi? Pingu can do many things such as swimming across the ocean and hiking across huge mountains. Let's find out more!

Modal Verbs

In this chapter, my goal is to provide you with the tools you need to discuss Modal verbs in Hindi. Such verbs are used to express ability, possibility, permission, obligation etc. You will be learning about the following modal verbs:

English	Hindi	Devanagari
Can	Saknā	सकना
Could	Sakā/ Sakī/ Sake	सका/ सकी/ सके
May	Saknā	सकना
Want	Chāhnā	चाहना
Should	Chāhiye	चाहिए

Modal Verb: Can

The verb can is used to say that *someone* is able to do *something*.

Examples include:

- I can teach Hindi.
- I can speak French.

The Hindi verb for "can" is "Saknā". In the prior classes, we learned the following:

- I speak Hindi.
- Maĩ Hindī boltā hū̃.
- मैं हिन्दी बोलता हूँ ।

Now imagine that you want to convey "I can speak." First, let's see how we say "I can". It will be "Maĩ saktā/saktī hū̃". Now, if you want to say "I can speak", put the base stem of bolnā (bol) before "saktā/saktī". The sentence would be "Maĩ bol saktā hū̃ *(male)*."

Following are the rules for verb conjugation for the modal verb "saknā".

Subject	Verb Conjugation (Chalnā)	Saknā (conjugation)	Rules
Maĩ	Chal	Saktā hũ. Saktī hũ.	Replace "nā" in the modal verb with "tā". Replace "nā" in the modal verb with "tī".
Tum	Chal	Sakte ho. Saktī ho.	Replace "nā" in the modal verb with "te". Replace "nā" in the modal verb with "tī".
Tū Vah / Yah	Chal	Saktā hai. Saktī hai.	Replace "nā" in the modal verb with "tā". Replace "nā" in the modal verb with "tī".
Hum Āp Ve / Ye	Chal	Sakte haĩ. Saktī haĩ.	Replace "nā" in the modal verb with "te". Replace "nā" in the modal verb with "tī".

You will notice that in all the above sentences the base stem of the verb "chal" is used without modification, regardless of the pronoun.

- I can walk. *(male)*
- Maĩ chal saktā hũ. *(male)*
- मैं चल सकता हूँ ।

- I can walk. *(female)*
- Maĩ chal saktī hũ. *(female)*
- मैं चल सकती हूँ ।

- You (familiar) can walk.
- Tum chal sakte ho. *(male)*
- तुम चल सकते हो ।

- You (intimate) can walk.
- Tū chal saktā hai. *(male)*
- तू चल सकता है ।

- He can walk.
- Vah chal saktā hai.
- वह चल सकता है ।

- She can walk.
- Vah chal saktī hai.
- वह चल सकती है ।

- We can walk.
- You can walk.
- They can walk.

- Hum chal sakte haĩ.
- हम चल सकते हैं।
- Āp chal sakte haĩ.
- आप चल सकते हैं।
- Ve chal sakte haĩ.
- वे चल सकते हैं।

Exercise 10.1 Help Pingu complete the following sentences (_____ *can write in Hindi*) (likhnā लिखना = to write)

1. Maĩ Hindī mẽ _____ . *(male)*
2. Maĩ Hindī mẽ _____ . *(female)*
3. Āp Hindī mẽ _____ .
4. Hum Hindī mẽ _____ .
5. Ve Hindī mẽ _____ .
6. Vah Hindī mẽ _____ . *(male)*
7. Vah Hindī mẽ _____ . *(female)*

१ मैं हिन्दी में _____ । *(male)*
२ मैं हिन्दी में _____ । *(female)*
३ आप हिन्दी में _____ ।
४ हम हिन्दी में _____ ।
५ वे हिन्दी में _____ ।
६ वह हिन्दी में _____ । *(male)*
७ वह हिन्दी में _____ । *(female)*

Exercise 10.2 Help Pingu translate the following sentences in Hindi.

1. I can play professional cricket.
2. They can drive for 10 hours.
3. We can speak and write 10 languages fluently.
4. You can work non-stop for 12 hours.
5. He can develop a software program in 5 days.
6. She can knit a sweater in 2 days.

<u>More complex examples</u>:

- What can I do for you? *(male)*
- Maĩ āpke liye kyā kar saktā hũ?
- मैं आपके लिये क्या कर सकता हूँ ?

- I can go to India this year. *(male)*
- Maĩ is sāl India jā saktā hũ.
- मैं इस साल India जा सकता हूँ ।

- I can speak Hindi a little bit. *(female)*
- Maĩ thodī Hindī bol saktī hũ.
- मैं थोड़ी हिन्दी बोल सकती हूँ ।

- Can you teach me Hindi?
- Kyā āp mujhe Hindī sikhā sakte haĩ?
- क्या आप मुझे हिन्दी सिखा सकते हैं ?

- I can't help you.
- Maĩ āpkī madad nahī̃ kar saktā hũ.
- मैं आपकी मदद नहीं कर सकता हूँ ।

- They can't perform today.
- Ve āj perform nahī̃ kar sakte haĩ.
- वे आज perform नहीं कर सकते हैं ।

- We can't do this.
- Hum yah nahī̃ kar sakte haĩ.
- हम यह नहीं कर सकते हैं ।

Modal Verb: Could

"Could" is a modal verb used to express a possibility, or a past ability, or to make suggestions and requests:

- I can walk = Maĩ chal saktā hũ *(male)*
- I could walk = Maĩ chal saktā tha *(male)*

In order to use "could" in negative sentences, you will be using the past form of saknā and conjugate it as "sakā/sakī/sake" based on the pronoun used.

Below are the rules for the verb conjugation (Example: I couldn't speak)

Subject	Verb Conjugation (Bolnā)	Not	Form of Saknā	Rules
Maĩ	Bol	Nahī̃	Sakā. *(male)* Sakī. *(female)*	replace "nā" with "ā". replace "nā" with "ī".
Tum			Sake. *(male)* Sakī. *(female)*	replace "nā" with "e". replace "nā" with "ī".
Tū Vah / Yah			Sakā. *(male)* Sakī. *(female)*	replace "nā" with "ā". replace "nā" with "ī".
Āp Hum Ve / Ye			Sake. *(male)* Sakī. *(female)*	replace "nā" with "e". replace "nā" with "ī".

These sentences <u>will not</u> end with "hai" or any other forms of "to be".

- I couldn't speak. *(male)*
- Maĩ bol nahī̃ sakā. *(male)*
- मैं बोल नहीं सका ।

- I couldn't speak. *(female)*
- Maĩ bol nahī̃ sakī. *(female)*
- मैं बोल नहीं सकी ।

- You (familiar) couldn't walk.
- Tum chal nahī̃ sake. *(male)*
- तुम चल नहीं सके ।

- You (intimate) couldn't walk.
- Tū chal nahī̃ sakā. *(male)*
- तू चल नहीं सका ।

- He couldn't walk.
- Vah chal nahī̃ sakā.
- वह चल नहीं सका ।

- She couldn't walk.
- Vah chal nahī̃ sakī.
- वह चल नहीं सकी ।

- We couldn't walk.
- You couldn't walk.
- They couldn't walk.

- Hum chal nahī̃ sake.
- हम चल नहीं सके ।
- Āp chal nahī̃ sake.
- आप चल नहीं सके ।
- Ve chal nahī̃ sake.
- वे चल नहीं सके ।

More complex examples:

- I couldn't recognize you. *(male)*
- I couldn't eat spicy food. (female)
- We couldn't win.
- They couldn't go to Paris.
- She couldn't book her ticket on time.

- Maī̃ āpko pehchān nahī̃ sakā.
- मैं आपको पहचान नहीं सका ।
- Maī̃ spicy khānā nahī̃ khā sakī.
- मैं spicy खाना नहीं खा सकी ।
- Hum jīt nahī̃ sake.
- हम जीत नहीं सके ।
- Ve Paris nahī̃ jā sake.
- वे Paris नहीं जा सके ।
- Vah samay par apnā ticket book nahī̃ kar sakī.
- वह समय पर अपना टिकट नहीं book कर सकी ।

Modal Verb: May

May is used to express uncertainty, probability, possibility, and to express permission, desires, or wishes. In Hindi, you will continue to use the forms of "saknā" to seek permission (e.g., May I come in?)

- May I come? *(male)*
- May I come inside the office?

- Kyā maī̃ ā saktā hū̃? *(male)*
- क्या मैं आ सकता हूँ ?
- Kyā maī̃ office ke andar ā saktā hū̃?
- क्या मैं office के अंदर आ सकता हूँ ?

Modal Verb: To want

"To want" is actually a verb. It's called "chāhnā" in Hindi. It literally means you desire for something.

For example:

- I desire a coffee.   = Maĩ coffee chāhtā hũ. *(male)*
- I want a coffee.   मैं कॉफ़ी चाहता हूँ ।

It will follow the same verb conjugation you used for the present indefinite tense. However, if you use the verb "want" with another verb, it becomes a little interesting. For example:

- I want to drink coffee.
- मैं coffee पीना चाहता हूँ ।
- Maĩ coffee pīnā chāhtā hũ.

You will notice that we used the infinitive form of the verb "pīnā". "Pīnā" isn't conjugated here. Let's review more examples to understand the concept:

- You want to go.
- Do you want to go?
- I want to go. *(male)*

- Āp jānā chāhte haĩ.
- आप जाना चाहते हैं ।
- Kyā āp jānā chāhte haĩ?
- क्या आप जाना चाहते हैं ?
- Maĩ jānā chāhtā hũ. *(male)*
- मैं जाना चाहता हूँ ।

Modal Verb: Should

The modal verb "should" is used mainly to give advice or to make recommendations, to talk about obligation or about probability and expectation. This modal verb follows a different pattern. You will notice:

- Use of postposition "Ko" with all the pronouns.
- Should is translated as "Chāhiye" चाहिए in Hindi
- Verbs are used in the infinitive form (e.g., to go = jānā जाना, to speak = bolnā बोलना)

Let's look at an example:

- You should go.

In this case:

- You = Āp
- To go = Jānā (infinitive form of the verb)
- Should = Chāhiye

So our final sentence will be:

- Āp + Jānā + Chāhiye
- आप + जाना + चाहिए

Are we missing anything here? Yes, you got it. A post-position "Ko" is missing after the pronoun. The postposition "Ko" is covered in detail in the next chapter.

Āp + Ko + Jānā + Chāhiye = Āpko jānā chāhiye. (आपको जाना चाहिए ।)

Let's look at more examples:

• You should eat.	• Āpko khānā chāhiye. • आपको खाना चाहिए ।
• You should sleep.	• Āpko sonā chāhiye. • आपको सोना चाहिए ।
• What should I do now?	• Ab mujhko kyā karnā chāhiye? • अब मुझको क्या करना चाहिए ?
• Should I go?	• Kyā mujhko jānā chāhiye? • क्या मुझको जाना चाहिए ?

Now that you have mastered the use of modals in Hindi, let's see how the modal verbs can be used in real life scenarios.

Scenario 1: Doctor's advice to a patient

- You should get up early.
- And you should exercise.
- You should not eat cheese and fried food.
- You should take medicine on time.
- You should not get too angry.
- You should spend time with your family.
- You should take care of yourself.
- You should come to get regular check-ups.

- Āpko jaldī uthnā chāhiye.
- आपको जल्दी उठना चाहिए ।

- Aur āpko vyāyām karnā chāhiye.
- और आपको व्यायाम करना चाहिए ।

- Āpko cheese aur talā huā khānā nahī̃ khānā chāhiye.
- आपको cheese और तला हुआ खाना नहीं खाना चाहिए ।

- Āpko samay pe dawāī lenī chāhiye.
- आपको समय पे दवाई लेनी चाहिए ।

- Āpko zyādā gussā nahī̃ karnā chāhiye.
- आपको ज़्यादा गुस्सा नहीं करना चाहिए ।

- Āpko apne parivār ke sāth samay bitānā chāhiye.
- आपको अपने परिवार के साथ समय बिताना चाहिए ।

- Āpko apnā dhyān rakhnā chāhiye.
- आपको अपना ध्यान रखना चाहिए ।

- Āpko regular check-ups ke liye ānā chāhiye.
- आपको regular check-ups के लिये आना चाहिए ।

Scenario 2: Giving advice

- You should work more.
- You should study more.
- You should listen to your teacher.
- You should go to class on time.
- You should do your homework.
- You should not watch TV.
- You should laugh a lot.

- Āpko zyādā kām karnā chāhiye.
- आपको ज़्यादा काम करना चाहिए ।
- Āpko zyādā paḍhnā chāhiye.
- आपको ज़्यादा पढ़ना चाहिए ।
- Āpko teacher kī bāt sunnī chāhiye.
- आपको teacher की बात सुननी चाहिए ।
- Āpko class mẽ samay par jānā chāhiye.
- आपको क्लास में समय पर जाना चाहिए ।
- Āpko apnā gruh-kārya karnā chāhiye.
- आपको अपना गृह कार्य करना चाहिए ।
- Āpko TV nahī̃ dekhnī chāhiye.
- आपको TV नहीं देखनी चाहिए ।
- Āpko bahut hā̃snā chāhiye.
- आपको बहुत हँसना चाहिए ।

Exercise 10.3 Help Pingu fill in the blanks with the most suitable word.

chāhiye	chāhte	saktā	sakī	saktī	sakā

1 Maĩ āpkī madad kar _____ hū̃.
2 Maĩ usko dekh nahī̃ _____ .
3 Usko har din skūl jānā _____ .
4 Maĩ kitāb ko samay pe paḍh nahī̃ _____ .
5 Kyā āp kitāb paḍhnā _____ haĩ?
6 Vah bahut acchā nāch _____ hai.

१ मैं आपकी मदद कर _____ हूँ ।
२ मैं उसको देख नहीं _____ ।
३ उसको हर दिन स्कूल जाना _____ ।
४ मैं किताब को समय पे पढ़ नहीं _____ ।
५ क्या आप किताब पढ़ना _____ हैं ?
६ वह बहुत अच्छा नाच _____ है ।

Hindi Vocabulary

It's time to brush up on your vocabulary from this chapter.

English	Hindi	Devanagari
Apologize	Māfī mā̃gnā	माफी माँगना
Careful	Sāvdhān	सावधान
Exercise	Vyāyām	व्यायाम
Law	Kānūn	कानून
Rent	Kirāyā	किराया
Smoking	Nashā / Dhūmrapān	नशा / धूम्रपान
On time	Samay pe	समय पे
This year	Is sāl	इस साल
To take care	Dhyān rakhnā	ध्यान रखना
To teach	Sikhānā	सिखाना
To help	Madad Karnā	मदद करना
To recognize	Pahchānnā	पहचानना

Watch the video "Giving Advice" at YouTube.com/HindiUniversity (playlist: Pingu Learns To Speak Hindi) to deepen your learning.

Get inspired by HindiUniversity students

Lia (Spain)

Merā nām Lia hai. Maī bacchō kī kahāniyā̃ likhtī hū̃. Merī do ladkiyā̃ haī. Unko merī kahāniyā̃ bahut pasand haī. Maī unse unkī rāy pūchtī saktī hū̃ aur maī lucky hū̃ kyō ki ve hameshā sach boltī haī. Ve merī madad karnā chāhtī haī. Maī unke liye bahut sī kahāniyā̃ likhnā chāhtī hū̃. Maī sochtī hū̃ ki humko sāth sāth ek kahānī likhnī chāhiye ! Mujhe yakīn hai ki ham ek sāth bacchō ke liye acchī kahāniyā̃ likh sakte haī

मेरा नाम Lia है । मैं बच्चों की कहानियाँ लिखती हूँ । मेरी दो लड़कियाँ हैं । उनको मेरी कहानियाँ बहुत पसंद हैं । मैं उनसे उनकी राय पूछती हूँ और मैं lucky हूँ क्यों कि वे हमेशा सच बोलती हैं । वे मेरी मदद करना चाहती हैं । मैं उनके लिए बहुत सी कहानियाँ लिखना चाहती हूँ । मैं सोचती हूँ कि हमको साथ साथ एक कहानी लिखनी चाहिए ! मुझे यकीन है कि हम एक साथ बच्चों के लिए अच्छी कहानियाँ लिख सकते हैं ।

Maria (Casablanca)

Merā nām Maria hai. Maī skūl jā rahī hū̃. Mujhko Hindī bhāshā bahut pasand haī. Maī Hindī padhnā chāhtī hū̃. Hindī mushkil nahī̃ hai, lekin mujhko har din zyādā padhnā aur likhnā chāhiye. Maī bahut khush hū̃ kyō ki kal maīne apne adhyāpak ke sāth ek lambī bātchīt karī! Agle sāl maī India jānā chāhti hū̃.

मेरा नाम Maria है । मैं स्कूल जा रही हूँ । मुझको हिन्दी भाषा बहुत पसंद हैं ! मैं हिन्दी पढ़ना चाहती हूँ । हिन्दी मुश्किल नहीं है , लेकिन मुझको हर दिन ज़्यादा पढ़ना और लिखना चाहिए । मैं बहुत खुश हूँ क्यों कि कल मैंने अपने अध्यापक के साथ एक लंबी बातचीत करी ! अगले साल में India जाना चाहती हूँ ।

Chapter 11

Pingu is sitting on an iceberg

+ Pingu will learn more postpositions and be able to say what she needs, what she can do for you, and where she is sitting.

Hindi Postpositions

In the earlier chapters, we focused on some essential postpositions (se, mẽ, kā, ke, and kī). In this chapter, I want to introduce three more Hindi postpositions: "pe", "ke liye", "ko" and compound post-positions.

Postpostion: Pe/Par पे/पर (On)

The postposition "Pe" translates to "On" in English. Hindi speakers use "Pe" and "Par" interchangeably in a conversation.

Consider the following examples:

English	Hindi	Devanagari
On the table	Mez par	मेज पर
On the tree	Ped par	पेड़ पर
On the bridge	Bridge par	Bridge पर
On the roof	Chhat par	छत पर

Consider the following sentences:

- They were playing on the roof.
- A pen is on the table.
- The monkey is on the tree.
- She is walking on the bridge.
- He is writing on the wall.

- Ve chhat pe khel rahe the.
- वे छत पे खेल रहे थे ।

- Kalam mez pe hai.
- क़लम मेज़ पे है ।

- Bandar ped pe hai.
- बंदर पेड़ पे है ।

- Vah bridge pe chal rahī hai.
- वह bridge पे चल रही है ।

- Vah dīwār pe likh rahā hai.
- वह दीवार पे लिख रहा है ।

Let's see how the pronouns are modified when we use them with the postposition "Pe".

English	Hindi	Devanagari
On me	Mujh pe	मुझ पे
On you	Tum pe	तुम पे
On you (informal)	Tujh pe	तुझ पे
On him/her/that	Us pe	उस पे
On this	Is pe	इस पे
On us	Hum pe	हम पे
On you (formal)	Āp pe	आप पे
On them/those	Un pe	उन पे
On these	In pe	इन पे
On who	Kis pe	किस पे

Consider the following sentences:

- The mother puts oil on the baby.
- The doctor puts ointment on the patients.

- Mā̃ bacche pe tel lagātī hai.
- माँ बच्चे पे तेल लगाती है ।
- Doctor marīzō pe marham lagātā hai.
- डॉक्टर मरीजों पे मरहम लगाता है ।

In the above examples, the verb is "lagana", which means to "to put" or "to apply"

Postpostion: Ke liye के लिए (For)

The post-position "Ke liye" translates to "for" in English. It doesn't change based on the gender of the nouns.

Consider the following examples:

English	Hindī	Devanagari
For society	Samāz ke liye	समाज़ के लिए
For example	Udāharan ke liye	उदाहरण के लिए
For now	Abhī ke liye	अभी के लिए
For peace	Shānti ke liye	शांति के लिए

Consider the following sentences:

- I want to work for society.
- She is praying for peace.

- Mai samāz ke liye kām karnā chāhtā hū̃.
- मैं समाज़ के लिए काम करना चाहता हूँ ।
- Vah shānti ke liye prayer kar rahī hai.
- वह शांति के लिए prayer कर रही है ।

Let's see how the pronouns get modified when we use them with the postposition "Ke liye".

English	Hindi	Devanagari
For me	Mere liye	मेरे लिए
For you	Tumhāre liye	तुम्हारे लिए
For you	Tere liye	तेरे लिए
For him/her/that	Uske liye	उसके लिए
For this	Iske liye	इसके लिए
For us	Humāre liye	हमारे लिए
For you	Āpke liye	आपके लिए
For them/those	Unke liye	उनके लिए
For these	Inke liye	इनके लिए
For who	Kiske liye	किसके लिए

Consider the following sentences:

- He is making tea for me.
- This isn't for me.
- This is difficult for him.

- Vah mere liye chāy banā rahā hai.
- वह मेरे लिए चाय बना रहा है ।
- Yah mere liye nahī̃ hai.
- यह मेरे लिए नहीं है ।
- Yah uske liye mushkil hai.
- यह उसके लिए मुश्किल है ।

Postpostion: Ko को (to)

The postposition "Ko" roughly translates to "to" in English. I will be covering five types of sentences where you can use the postposition "Ko". Review the table below and see how the pronouns will be modified when we use them with "Ko".

Pronouns	Post-position	Outcome	Meaning
Maĩ मैं		Mujko मुझको	To me
Tum तुम		Tumko तुमको	To you
Tū तू		Tujhko तुझको	To you
Vah वह	+ ko को	Usko उसको	To him/her/that
Yah यह		Isko इसको	To this
Hum हम		Humko हमको	To us
Āp आप		Āpko आपको	To you
Ve वे		Unko उनको	To them
Ye ये		Inko इनको	To these

As you probably noticed above, the pronouns are getting modified.

Maĩ मैं + ko को = mujhko मुझको (to me)
Tū तू + ko को = tujhko तुझको (to you)

143

The same goes for other pronouns. Now let's see how these modified pronouns can be used in several Hindi sentences.

Type 1: If you need something

In such sentences, you want to say, "I need ___ ."

Consider the following examples:

- I need help.
- I need ice-cream.
- I need a job.
- I need money.
- I need love.

In Hindi, this roughly translates to:

- To me _____ is needed.
  (I need _____)
- Mujhko _____ chāhiye.
  मुझको _____ चाहिए ।

Let's try to practice "Ko" with some examples. Review the template above and make Hindi sentences.

Aren't you surprised how easy it is to formulate so many sentences!

- I need help.
- Mujhko madad chāhiye.
- मुझको मदद चाहिए ।

- They need medicine.
- Unko dawāī chāhiye.
- उनको दवाई चाहिए ।

- She needs a rickshaw.
- Usko rickshāw chāhiye.
- उसको रिक्शा चाहिए ।

- He needs food.
- Usko khānā chāhiye.
- उसको खाना चाहिए ।

- We need love.
- Humko pyār chāhiye.
- हमको प्यार चाहिए ।

- You need work.
- He/she needs water.

- Tumko kām chāhiye.
- तुमको काम चाहिए ।

- Usko pānī chāhiye.
- उसको पानी चाहिए ।

Type 2: If you like someone or something

If you like a particular person, place, or thing, you can use "Ko" and express it in Hindi.

Consider the following examples:

- I like ice-cream.
- I like biking.
- I like the movie.
- I like Peru.

In Hindi, this roughly translates to:

- To me _____ is liked.
  (I like _____)
- Mujhko _____ pasand hai.
  मुझको _____ पसंद है ।

Let's practice making sentences using the formula above:

- Mujhko ice-cream pasand hai.
- मुझको ice-cream पसंद है ।

- Unko shor pasand nahī̃ hai.
- उनको शोर पसंद नहीं है ।

- Āpko kyā pasand hai?
- आपको क्या पसंद है ?

- Kyā tumko Bollywood movies pasand hai?
- क्या तुमको Bollywood movies पसंद है ?

- John ko ghūmnā pasand hai.
- John को घूमना पसंद है ।

Type 3: If you have a particular symptom

If you have a particular health condition, you can use "Ko" and express it in Hindi.

Consider the following examples:

- I have a fever.
- I have a stomach ache.
- I have a cold.
- I have fear.

In Hindi, this roughly translates to:

- To me _____ has arrived / happened. (I have _____)
- Mujhko _____ hai.
  मुझको _____ है ।

Let's practice making some sentences using the formula above:

- I have a fever.
  - Mujhko bukhār hai.
  - मुझको बुखार है ।

- You have a headache.
  - Āpko sir dard hai.
  - आपको सिर दर्द है ।

- She has a stomach ache.
  - Usko pet dard hai.
  - उसको पेट दर्द है ।

- He has a toothache.
  - Usko dā̃t mẽ dard hai.
  - उसको दाँत में दर्द है ।

- We have chronic pain.
  - Humko chronic pain hai.
  - हमको chronic pain है ।

- They have a cold.
  - Unko sardī hai.
  - उनको सर्दी है ।

Type 4: You have information about something

If you have knowledge/information about something, you can use "Ko" to express it in Hindi.

Consider the following examples:

- I know Hindi.
- I don't know this.
- I know cooking.
- I know swimming.

In Hindi, this roughly translates to:

- To me _____ is known.
  I know _____ .
- Mujhko mālūm / patā hai.
  मुझको मालूम / पता है ।

Let's practice making some sentences using the formula above:

- I know.
- Mujhko mālūm hai.
- मुझको मालूम है ।

- She knows. / She is aware.
- Usko patā hai.
- उसको पता है ।

- He doesn't know.
- Usko nahī̃ patā hai.
- उसको नहीं पता है ।

- They know cooking.
- Unko cooking ātī hai.
- उनको खाना बनाना आता है ।

- You know cooking.
- Tumko cooking ātī hai.
- तुमको खाना बनाना आता है ।

- You know swimming.
- Āpko swimming ātī hai.
- आपको swimming आती है ।

Type 5: To describe abstract nouns

You can express feelings, mood, and faith (abstract nouns) with "Ko".

Consider the following examples:

- I have faith.
- I am happy.
- I have hope.

In Hindi, this roughly translates to:

- To me _____ exists.
  (I have _____) (Abstract nouns)
- Mujhko _____ hai.
  मुझको _____ है ।

Let's practice making some sentences using the formula above:

- I'm happy.
  - Mujhko khushī hai.
  - मुझको खुशी है ।

- I have hope.
  - Mujhko ummīd hai.
  - मुझको उम्मीद है ।

- I have faith/hope.
  - Mujhko āshā hai.
  - मुझको आशा है ।

- I have trouble.
  - Mujhko pareshānī hai.
  - मुझको परेशानी है ।

- I'm sad.
  - Mujhko dukh hai.
  - मुझको दुःख है ।

- I'm proud.
  - Mujhko garv hai.
  - मुझको गर्व है ।

> Watch the video "Postposition: ko" at YouTube.com/HindiUniversity (playlist: Pingu Learns To Speak Hindi) to deepen your learning.

Exercise 11.1 Help Pingu choose the correct word to complete the sentences.

unko	unke liye	pe	usko	tumhāre liye

1 Billī mez _____ hai.
2 Vah _____ rotī banā rahī hai
3 Tum _____ gānā likh rahe ho.
4 _____ kitābẽ bahut pasand hai.
5 _____ bahut khushī hai.

१ बिल्ली मेज़ _____ है ।
२ वह _____ रोटी बना रही है ।
३ तुम _____ गाना लिख रहे हो ।
४ _____ किताबें बहुत पसंद है ।
५ _____ बहुत ख़ुशी है ।

Exercise 11.2 Help Pingu translate the following sentences in Hindi.

1 I am sitting on the bed. *(male)*
2 We are singing a song for her.
3 She has a fever. She needs medicine.
4 You like Hindi stories very much.
5 They know how to cook food.
6 She is waiting for him.
7 You have hope.

Exercise 11.3 Help Pingu change the sentences in exercise 11.2 into the interrogative (*i.e., Did you sit on the chair?*)

Exercise 11.4 Each sentence has an error; help Pingu find it and correct it!

1 Kyā āp kursī liye nahī̃ baithe?
2 Kyā ve uske pe kahānī nahī̃ likh rahe hai?
3 Kyā vah abhī ke liye kām kar rahā hai?
4 Kyā āp dawāī nahī̃ chāhiye?
5 Kyā Un ummīd hai?
6 Kyā tum Address mālūm nahī̃ hai?
7 Kyā Us ice-cream hai?

१ क्या आप कुर्सी लिए नहीं बैठे?
२ क्या वे उसके पे कहानी को नहीं लिख रहे है ?
३ क्या वह अभी के लिए काम कर रहा है ?
४ क्या आप दवाई नहीं चाहिए ?
५ क्या उन उम्मीद है ?
६ क्या तुम Address मालूम नहीं है ?
७ क्या उस ice-cream पसंद है ?

Postpositions after nouns

In Hindi, there are two cases, the Direct case and the Oblique case. When a word is used with a postposition, it is in the Oblique case. In all other cases, it is in the Direct case. In this section, you will learn how the nouns get modified when they are used with a postposition. Let's review Hindi postpositions using the tables below.

Postpositions		
English	Hindi	Devanagari
From/Of/By	Se	से
In	Mẽ	में
On	Pe/Par	पे / पर
For	Ke Liye	के लिए
To	Ko	को
's	Kā / Kī / Ke	का / की / के

Compound Postpositions		
English	Hindi	Devanagari
Behind	Ke pīche	के पीछे
On top of	Ke ūpar	के ऊपर
Below	Ke nīche	के नीचे
Before	Se pehle	से पहले
After	Ke bād	के बाद
Near	Ke pās	के पास
With	Ke sāth	के साथ
About	Ke bāre mẽ	के बारे में
Inside	Ke andar	के अंदर
Outside	Ke bāhar	के बाहर

The postposition modifies the preceding noun based on the noun's gender and its number (i.e., singular vs plural).

In the following section, we will go over this rule in more detail.

Rule 1: Postposition after masculine singular nouns:

Masculine Singular Nouns	
Marked Nouns	**Unmarked Nouns**
• Marked nouns end with "ā" • When you add a postposition, the ending changes to the "e" sound. Example: Betā + Ko = bete ko बेटा + को = बेटे को (to the son) Kamrā + mẽ = kamre mẽ कमरा + में = कमरे में (in the room)	• All other masculine nouns which <u>do not</u> end with "ā" • When you add a postposition, the ending doesn't change. Example: Ped + se = Ped se पेड़ + से = पेड़ से (from the tree) ghar + ke andar = ghar ke andar घर + के अंदर = घर के अंदर (in the house)

Rule 2: Postposition after masculine plural nouns:

Masculine Plural Nouns	
Plural of Marked Nouns	**Plural of Unmarked Nouns**
• The plural of Marked nouns end with "e" • When you add a postposition, the ending "e" changes to the "õ" sound. Example: Bete + Ke Liye = betõ ke Liye बेटे + के लिए = बेटों के लिए (for the sons) Kamre + mẽ = kamrõ mẽ कमरे + में = कमरों में (in the rooms)	• The plural of Unmarked nouns is the same as the singular. • When you add a postposition, the ending changes to the "õ" sound. Example: Ped + se = Pedõ se पेड़ + से = पेड़ों से (from the trees) ghar + ke andar = gharõ ke andar घर + के अंदर = घरों के अंदर (in the houses)

Exercise 11.5 Help Pingu write the correct form of the nouns in the brackets taking into account the postposition.

1. _____ ke nīche (kapdā)
2. _____ Ke nīche (kalam)
3. _____ ke liye (chāchā)
4. _____ se (ladkā)

१. _____ के नीचे (कपड़ा)
२. _____ के नीचे (क़लम)
३. _____ के लिए (चाचा)
४. _____ से (लड़का)

Exercise 11.6 Help Pingu translate the sentences in Hindi.

1. The cat is on the tree.
2. She is afraid of dogs.
3. My brother is behind the door.
4. Is your book near the desk?

Rule 3: Postposition after feminine singular nouns:

Feminine singular Nouns	
Marked Nouns	**Unmarked Nouns**
• Marked nouns end with "ī". • When you make a plural, the word doesn't change. Example: Ladkī + ko = ladkī ko लड़की + को = लड़की को (to the girl) Nadī + ke pās = nadī ke pās नदी + के पास = नदी के पास (near the river)	• All other feminine nouns which do not end with "ī". • When you make a plural, the word doesn't change. Example: Kitāb + mẽ = Kitāb mẽ किताब + में = किताब में (in the book) Mez + par = Mez par मेज़ + पर = मेज़ पर (on the table)

Rule 4: Postposition after feminine plural nouns:

Feminine Plural Nouns	
Plural of Marked Nouns	**Plural of Unmarked Nouns**
• The plural of Marked nouns end with "iyã" • When you add a postposition, the ending "iyã" changes to the "iyõ" sound. Examples: Ladkiyã + ko = ladkiyõ ko लड़कियाँ + को = लड़कियों को (to the girls) Nadīyã + ke pās = nadiyõ ke pās नदियाँ + के पास = नदियों के पास (near the rivers)	• The plural of Unmarked nouns end with "ẽ" • When you add a postposition, the ending "ẽ" changes to the "õ" sound. Example: Kitābẽ + mẽ = Kitābõ mẽ किताबें + में = किताबों में (in the books) Mezẽ + par = Mezõ par मेज़ें + पर = मेज़ों पर (on the tables)

Exercise 11.7 Help Pingu decide the correct form of the nouns.

1 Bahanẽ + ke liye = _____
2 Mezẽ + par = _____
3 Bhāshāẽ + ke bāre mẽ = _____
4 Topīyã + pe = _____

१ बहनें + के लिए = _____ ।
२ मेज़ें + पर = _____ ।
३ भाषाएँ + के बारे में = _____ ।
४ टोपियाँ + पे = _____ ।

Exercise 11.8 Help Pingu translate the following sentences in Hindi.

1 He is in the car.
2 The glasses are on the table.
3 Her friend is talking about the stories.
4 Will you sleep after the movie?

Exercises 11.9 Help Pingu look at the picture and write where everything is.

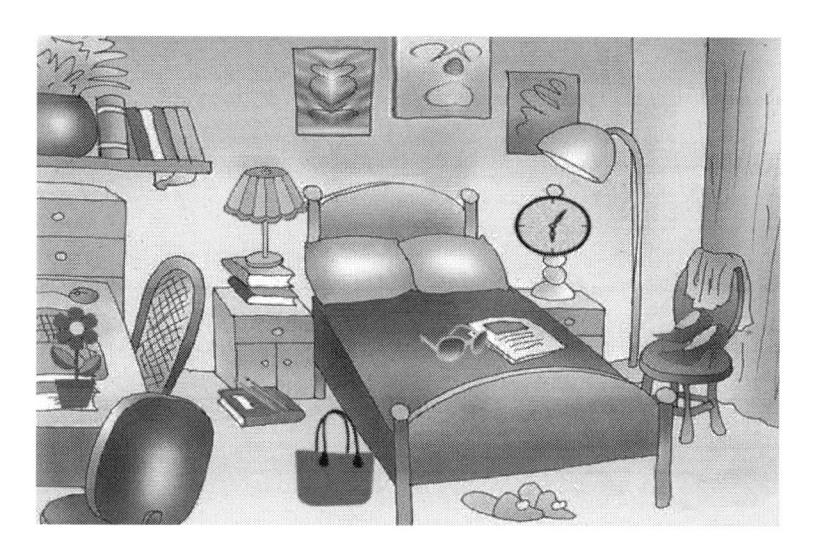

1 Jūte, kursī ___par___ haĩ.
2 Chashmā, akhbār _____ hai.
3 Akhbār, bistar _____ hai.
4 Phul, mez _____ hai.
5 Lamp, kitābõ _____ hai.
6 Bag, bistar _____ haĩ.
7 Do pencils, kitāb _____ haĩ.
8 Tīn tasvīrẽ, dīvār _____ haĩ.
9 Chappalẽ, bistar _____ haĩ.
10 Ghadī, darāz _____ hai.

१ जूते, कुर्सी ___पर___ हैं।
२ चश्मा अख़बार _____ है।
३ अख़बार बिस्तर _____ है।
४ फूल मेज़ _____ है।
५ Lamp किताबों _____ है।
६ Bag बिस्तर _____ है।
७ दो pencils किताब _____ हैं।
८ तीन तस्वीरें दीवार _____ हैं।
९ चप्पलें बिस्तर _____ हैं।
१० घडी दराज़ _____ है।

Exercise 11.10 Help Pingu fill-in the blanks with a suitable compound postposition.

| ke sāth | mere liye | ke ūpar | ke andar | ke bāhar | ke pās |

1 Meri jeb _____ āpkī chābiyā̃ haĩ.
2 Uske ghar _____ ek sundar bagīchā hai.
3 Vah _____ acchī chāy banātī hai.
4 Unke shehar _____ ek lambī nadī hai.
5 Maĩ Ady _____ Hindī kā homework karũgī.
6 Tumharī gadī _____ ek chhotī billī hai.

१ मेरे जेब _____ आपकी चाबियाँ हैं ।
२ उसके घर _____ एक सुंदर बगीचा है ।
३ वह _____ अच्छी चाय बनाती है ।
४ उनके शहर _____ एक लंबी नदी है ।
५ मैं Ady _____ हिन्दी का homework करूँगी ।
६ तुम्हारी गाड़ी _____ एक छोटी बिल्ली है ।

> Watch the video "Hindi Postposition" at YouTube.com/HindiUniversity (playlist: Pingu Learns To Speak Hindi) to deepen your learning.

Post positions after pronouns

You have learned about pronouns and postpositions in the earlier chapters. Now, you will learn how pronouns get modified when they are used with the postpositions. See the table below:

Pronouns			
Pronouns + postposition		**Result**	**Example (se)**
Maĩ मैं	+ postposition	Mujh मुझ	Mujh se मुझ से
Tum तुम		Tum तुम	Tum se तुम से
Tū तू		Tujh तुझ	Tujh se तुझ से
Vah वह		Us उस	Us se उस से
Yah यह		Is इस	Is se इस से
Hum हम		Hum हम	Hum se हम से
Āp आप		Āp आप	Āp se आप से
Ve वे		Un उन	Un se उन से
Ye ये		In इन	In se इन से

155

In this case, Kā/Ki/Ke postpositions follow a different pattern when used with pronouns. Let's see how:

- Maĩ + Kā /Kī/ Ke = merā/ merī/ mere
- Tū + Kā/Kī/Ke = terā/ terī/ tere
- Tum + Kā/Kī/Ke = tumhārā/ tumhārī/ tumhāre
- Hum + Kā/Kī/Ke = humārā/ humārī/ humāre

- मैं + का / की / के = मेरा / मेरी / मेरे
- तू + का / की / के = तेरा / तेरी / तेरे
- तुम + का / की / के = तुम्हारा / तुम्हारी / तुम्हारे
- हम + का / की / के = हमारा / हमारी / हमारे

Exercises 11.11 Help Pingu combine the pronouns with the postpositions and write the correct form.

1 Maĩ + ko = _____
2 Vah + mẽ = _____
3 Tum + se = _____
4 Hum + kī = _____
5 Tum + ke bāre mẽ = _____
6 Tū + ke liye = _____
7 Ve + ke bāhar = _____
8 Āp + ke sāth = _____

१ मैं + को = _____
२ वह + में = _____
३ तुम + से = _____
४ हम + की = _____
५ तुम + के बारे में = _____
६ तू + के लिए = _____
७ वे + के बाहर = _____
८ आप + के साथ = _____

Hindi Vocabulary

English	Hindi	Devanagari
Roof	Chhat	छत
Wall	Dīwār	दीवार
Floor	Farsh	फर्श
Floor rug	Darī	दरी
Chair	Kursī	कुर्सी
Bed	Palang	पलंग
Peace	Shā̃ti	शाँति
Medicine	Dawāī	दवाई
Love	Pyār	प्यार
Noise	Shor	शोर
Health	Tabiyat	तबियत
Fever	Bukhār	बुखार
Headache	Sir dard	सिर दर्द
Cold	Sardī	सर्दी
Song	Gīt / Gānā	गीत / गाना
Trouble	Pareshānī	परेशानी
Hope / Faith	Ummīd / Āshā	उम्मीद / आशा
To sing	Gānā	गाना
To play a game	Khelnā	खेलना
To run	Daudnā	दौड़ना

Conversation Between Kevin and Maddy

Kevin: Namaste. Āp kaise haĩ?
नमस्ते। आप कैसे हैं ?

Maddy: Namaste. Maĩ thīk hũ, shukriyā. Aur āp kaise haĩ?
नमस्ते. मैं ठीक हूँ, शुक्रिया। और आप कैसे हैं ?

Kevin: Merī tabiyat acchī nahī̃ hai. Mujhko bukhār hai.
मेरी तबियत अच्छी नहीं है । मुझको बुखार है ।

Maddy: Kyā āpko dawāī chāhiye?
क्या आपको दवाई चाहिए ?

Kevin: Hā̃, kyā āpko patā hai ki store kahā̃ hai?
हाँ, क्या आपको पता है कि store कहाँ है ?

Maddy: Hā̃, mujhko patā hai, aspatāl ke pās hai.
हाँ, मुझको पता है, अस्पताल के पास है ।

Kevin to Store Keeper: Bhaiyā, mujhko davāī kharīdnī hai.
भैया, मुझको दवाई खरीदनी है ।

Store Keeper: Āpko yah dawāī pānī ke sāth lenī hai. Mujhko ummīd hai, āp kal tak thīk ho jāoge.
आपको यह दवाई पानी के साथ लेनी है । मुझको उम्मीद है, आप कल तक ठीक हो जाओगे ।

Get inspired by HindiUniversity students

Your goal after completing Chapter 11 is to use postpositions in Hindi. See some of the writings from HindiUniversity students and get inspired.

Cecilia (Romania)

Merā nām Cecilia hai. Maĩ abhī mere mā-bāp ke sāth Norway mẽ rehtī hũ. Humāre ghar ke bāhar ek baḍā peḍ hai aur peḍ pe hameshā ek chiriyā gānā gātī hai. Merī mā̃ har subah mere liye chāy aur nāshtā banātī hai aur maĩ ghar sāf kartī hū̃. Maĩ agle mahīne nayā kām shuru karũgī islie mujhe apnā ghar chāhiye. Mujhko thoḍā dukh hai, lekin mujhko mālūm hai ki sab kuch acchā hogā !

मेरा नाम Cecilia है । मैं अभी मेरे माँ-बाप के साथ Norway में रहती हूँ। हमारे घर के बाहर एक बड़ा पेड़ है और पेड़ पे हमेशा एक चिड़िया गाना गाती है । मेरी माँ हर सुबह मेरे लिए चाय और नाश्ता बनाती है और मैं घर साफ करती हूँ । मैं अगले महीने नया काम शुरू करूँगी , इसलिए मुझे अपना घर चाहिए । मुझको थोड़ा दुःख है, लेकिन मुझको मालूम है कि सब कुछ अच्छा होगा !

Navaneeth (California, USA)

Merā nām Navaneeth hai. Maĩ chātr hū̃. Kal merā pehlā exam hai. Merī mez pe bahut se kāgaz aur kitābẽ haĩ. Maĩ purrī rāt paḍhā kyõ ki maĩ kakshā mẽ ek acchā aur smārt chātr bannā chāhtā hū̃. Merī mā̃ ne mere liye coffee aur snacks banāye. Mujhko sir dard hai aur mujhko dawāī chāhiye. Maĩ nashte ke bād paḍhtā rahũgā. Merī mā̃ bahut khush hogī !

मेरा नाम Navaneeth है। मैं छात्र हूँ। कल मेरा पहला exam है । मेरी मेज़ पे बहुत से कागज़ और किताबें हैं। मैं पूरी रात पढ़ा क्यों कि मैं कक्षा में एक अच्छा और smart छात्र बनना चाहता हूँ। मेरी माँ ने मेरे लिए coffee और snacks बनाये। मुझको सिर दर्द है और मुझको दवाई चाहिए। मैं नाश्ते के बाद पढ़ता रहूँगा ! मेरी माँ बहुत खुश होगी !

Chapter 12
Pingu asks questions

+ Pingu will be able to ask questions such as "Where are you?", "Who are you?", "What are you doing?" and Why are you doing it?

Hindi Interrogatives

In this chapter, I will cover Hindi Interrogatives. An interrogative is used to ask questions, such as what, when, where, who, whom, why, and how. They are sometimes called wh-words because, in English, most of them start with wh- (compare Five Ws). [Wikipedia]

In Hindi, all the interrogatives start with the sound "Ka" क . See the table below:

English interrogatives	Hindi Interrogatives	Devanagari
What	Kyā	क्या
Where	Kahā̃	कहाँ
How	Kaisā / Kaisī / Kaise	कैसा / कैसी / कैसे
When	Kab	कब
Who	Kaun	कौन
Which	Kaun sā / sī / se	कौन सा / सी / से
Why	Kyõ	क्यों

What - Kyā क्या

Do you recall the basic sentences we made using third-person pronouns (Yah, Vah, Ye, Ve)? I encourage you to review them before moving forward quickly.

You were able to say:

- This is a school.
- Yah skūl hai.
- यह स्कूल है ।

- That is a banana.
- These are vegetables.
- Those are pakoras. (Indian snacks)

- Vah kelā hai.
- वह केला है ।

- Ye sabjiyā̃ haĩ.
- ये सब्ज़ियाँ हैं ।

- Ve pakode haĩ.
- वे पकोड़े हैं ।

Now, imagine you see something new and want to inquire about it. How will you ask? Well, that's precisely where you will be using the interrogatives.

Subject	Interrogative	Linking Verbs (To be form)
Yah यह (this)	Kyā क्या (what)	hai है (is)
Vah वह (that)		hai है (is)
Ye ये (these)		haĩ हैं (are)
Ve वे (those)		haĩ हैं (are)

Case 1

- What is this?
- What is that?
- What are these?
- What are those?

- Yah kyā hai?
- यह क्या है ?

- Vah kyā hai?
- वह क्या है ?

- Ye kyā haĩ?
- ये क्या हैं ?

- Ve kyā haĩ?
- वे क्या हैं ?

The above four sentences can be powerful to initiate a conversation with someone in Hindi. Please note that if kyā is placed at the beginning of the sentence, it becomes a yes/no question (i.e., Kya yah table hai? Is this a table?)

Case 2

How about asking some more interesting questions like these below:

- What's your name?
- What's your qualification?
- What's your point?
- What's your strength?

If you recall from earlier chapters, we also learned about the use of postpositions "Kā", "Ke" and "Kī".

- His name
  - Uskā nām
  - उसका नाम

- Your qualification
  - Āpkī yogyatā
  - आपकी योग्यता

- Their point
  - Unkā matlab
  - उनका मतलब

- Her strength
  - Uskī tāqat
  - उसकी ताक़त

So you probably have guessed how to ask the above four questions in Hindi:

- Āpkā nām kyā hai?
- आपका नाम क्या है ?

- Āpkī yogyatā kyā hai?
- आपकी योग्यता क्या है ?

- Āpkā matlab kyā hai?
- आपका मतलब क्या है ?

- Āpkī strength kyā hai? (assuming you don't know how to say "strength" in Hindi)
- आपकी strength क्या है ?

To recap:

You - आप āp

Your - आपका āpkā (when followed by a masculine singular noun)

Your - आपकी āpkī   (when followed by a feminine singular noun)

- What is your _____?
- What is your phone number?
- What is your goal?
- What is your aim?
- What is your view?
- What is your favorite sport?
- What do you mean?
- What is your age?
- What is your strength?
- What's your weakness?

- Āpkā _____ kyā hai ?
- आपका _____ क्या है ?

- Āpkā phone number kyā hai?
- आपका phone number क्या है ?

- Āpkā maksad kyā hai?
- आपका मकसद क्या है ?

- Āpkā lakshya kyā hai?
- आपका लक्ष्य क्या है ?

- Āpkā mat kyā hai?
- आपका मत क्या है ?

- Āpkā pasandīdā khel kyā hai?
- आपका पसंदीदा खेल क्या है ?

- Āpkā matlab kyā hai?
- आपका मतलब क्या है ?

- Āpkī umr kyā hai?
- आपकी उम्र क्या है ?

- Āpkī tāqat kyā hai?
- आपकी ताक़त क्या है ?

- Āpkī kamzorī kyā hai?
- आपकी कमज़ोरी क्या है ?

Exercise 12.1 Help Pingu translate the following sentences in Hindi:

1. What's his address?
2. What's the matter?
3. What's her problem?
4. What's the question?
5. What's the answer?
6. What's the score?

Where - Kahā̃ कहाँ

You will be using the interrogative (Kahā̃) when you want to inquire where a particular person, place, or thing is. Let's review some cases.

Subject	Interrogative	Linking Verbs (To be form)
Yah यह (this)		hai है (is)
Vah वह (that)	Kahā̃ कहाँ (where)	hai है (is)
Ye ये (these)		haĩ हैं (are)
Ve वे (those)		haĩ हैं (are)

Case 1

- Where is this?
  - Yah kahā̃ hai?
  - यह कहाँ है ?

- Where is that?
  - Vah kahā̃ hai?
  - वह कहाँ है ?

- Where are these?
  - Ye kahā̃ haĩ?
  - ये कहाँ हैं ?

- Where are those?
- Ve kahā haĩ?
- वे कहाँ हैं ?

- Where is the train station?
- Train station kahā hai?
- Train station कहाँ है ?

- Where is the hospital?
- Hospital kahā hai?
- अस्पताल कहाँ है ?

Case 2

How about asking some interesting questions like these below:

- Where is your _____ ?
- Āpkā _____ kahā hai?
- आपका _____ कहाँ है ?

- Where is your shoe?
- Āpkā jūtā kahā hai?
- आपका जूता कहाँ है ?

- Where is your pen?
- Āpkī kalam kahā hai?
- आपकी क़लम कहाँ है ?

- Where is your city?
- Āpkā shehar kahā hai?
- आपका शहर कहाँ है ?

- Where is your home?
- Āpkā ghar kahā hai?
- आपका घर कहाँ है ?

- Where is your school?
- Āpkā vidhyālay kahā hai?
- आपका विद्यालय कहाँ है ?

- Where is your office?
- Āpkā daftar kahā hai?
- आपका दफ्तर कहाँ है ?

- Where is your family?
- Āpkā parivār kahā hai?
- आपका परिवार कहाँ है ?

- Where are you?
- Āp kahā̃ haĩ?
- आप कहाँ हैं ?

- Where do you live?
- Āp kahā̃ rehte haĩ?
- आप कहाँ रहते हैं ?

- Where is your car?
- Āpkī gāḍī kahā̃ hai?
- आपकी गाड़ी कहाँ है ?

- Where is your book?
- Āpkī kitāb kahā̃ hai?
- आपकी किताब कहाँ है ?

Exercise 12.2 Help Pingu translate the following sentences into Hindi:

1. Where is my passport?
2. Where are your keys?
3. Where are her glasses?
4. Where is the ceremony?

How - Kaisā कैसा / Kaisī कैसी / Kaise कैसे

You will be using this interrogative when you want to inquire about the well being, condition of someone, or a place. In Hindi, this interrogative is called "Kaisā", "Kaisī" or "Kaise" depending upon the gender of the subject.

Masculine Singular	Kaisā	कैसा
Masculine Plural	Kaise	कैसे
Feminine Singular	Kaisī	कैसी
Feminine Plural	Kaisī̃	कैसीं

Let's review some cases.

How is your ___ ?

- How is your work?
- How is your health?
- How is your mom?
- How is your life?
- How are your horse riding skills?
- How is your Hindi?

- Āpkā kām kaisā hai?
- आपका काम कैसा है ?

- Āpkī tabiyat kaisī hai?
- आपकी तबियत कैसी है ?

- Āpkī mā̃ kaisī haĩ?
- आपकी माँ कैसी है ?

- Āpkī zindagī kaisī hai?
- आपकी ज़िंदगी कैसी है ?

- Āpkī horse riding skills kaisī haĩ?
- आपकी horse riding skills कैसीं है ?

- Āpkī Hindī kaisī hai?
- आपकी हिन्दी कैसी है ?

Exercise 12.3 Help Pingu translate the following sentences into Hindi.

1 How are their families?
2 How was your vacation to Italy?
3 How was your weekend?
4 How is this class?

When - Kab कब

You will be using this interrogative (Kab) when you want to inquire about a particular event's timing. In Hindi, this interrogative is called "Kab". *Kab* stays the same regardless of the gender of the subject.

Let's review some cases.

- When is your game?
- Āpkā game kab hai?
- आपका game कब है ?

- When is her show?
- Uskā show kab hai?
- उसका show कब है ?

- When is his graduation?
- Uskī graduation kab hai?
- उसकी graduation कब है ?

- When is their wedding?
- Unkī shādī kab hai?
- उनकी शादी कब है ?

- When is your birthday?
- Āpkā janmadin kab hai?
- आपका जन्मदिन कब है ?

- When is her vacation?
- Uskī chhuttī kab hai?
- उसकी छुट्टी कब है ?

Exercise 12.4 Help Pingu translate the following sentences into Hindi.

1. When are they coming to town?
2. When will you go to Paris?
3. When do you practice Hindi?
4. When were you born? (Hint: To born = Paidā Honā पैदा होना - It's an irregular verb so you will be conjugating it accordingly)

Who - Kaun कौन

You will be using this interrogative when you want to inquire about the subject himself/herself. In Hindi, this interrogative is called "Kaun". *Kaun* stays the same regardless of the gender of the subject.

Let's review some cases.

- Who is _____ ?
- _____ kaun hai?
- _____ कौन है ?

- Who are you?
- Āp kaun haĩ?
- आप कौन हैं ?

- Who is coming to the party today?
- Āj party mẽ kaun ā rahā hai?
- आज party में कौन आ रहा है ?

- Who will run a marathon in the winter?
- Sardiyõ mẽ marathon kaun daudegā?
- सर्दियों में marathon कौन दौड़ेगा ?

- Who was crying yesterday?
- Kal kaun ro rahā thā?
- कल कौन रो रहा था ?

- Who can drive a car?
- Gādī kaun chalā saktā hai?
- गाड़ी कौन चला सकता है ?

Exercise 12.5 Help Pingu translate the following sentences into Hindi.

1. Who is Donald Trump?
2. Who can make tea?
3. Who came to your party yesterday?
4. Who knows the answers?

Which - Kaun sā कौन सा / Kaun se कौन से / Kaun sī कौन सी

You will be using this interrogative when you want to inquire about things. In Hindi, this interrogative is called "Kaun sā", "Kaun se", "Kaun sī", depending upon the gender of the thing in question.

As a rule of thumb: Use **which** for *things* and **who** for *people*

Masculine Singular	Kaun sā	कौन सा
Masculine Plural	Kaun se	कौन से
Feminine Singular/Plural	Kaun sī	कौन सी

Let's review some cases.

- Which airport?
  - Kaun sā airport?
  - कौन सा airport ?

- Which car?
  - Kaun sī car?
  - कौन सी car ?

- Which car do you drive?
  - Āp kaun sī gadī chalāte hai?
  - आप कौन सी गाड़ी चलाते हैं ?

- Which movie will you watch tonight?
  - Āp āj rāt kaun sī movie dekhẽge?
  - आप आज रात कौन सी movie देखेंगे ?

- Which book should I read?
  - Mujhko kaun sī kitāb padhnī chāhiye?
  - मुझको कौन सी किताब पढ़नी चाहिए ?

- Which hotel should I stay at in Delhi?
  - Mujhko Delhī mẽ kaun sī hotel mẽ theharnā chāhiye?
  - मुझको दिल्ली में कौन सी hotel में ठहरना चाहिए ?

Exercise 12.6 Help Pingu translate the following sentences into Hindi.

1. Which class?
2. Which train?
3. Which animal?
4. Which shoes should I buy?
5. Which medicine should I buy?
6. Which sport do you like?
7. Which language do you speak?

Why - Kyõ क्यों

You will be using this interrogative when you want to inquire about the reason for something. In Hindi, this interrogative is called "Kyõ". Kyõ stays the same regardless of the gender of the subject.

Let's review some cases:

- Why is the baby crying?
  - Bacchā kyõ ro rahā hai?
  - बच्चा क्यों रो रहा है ?

- Why can't I go to India?
  - Maĩ India kyõ nahĩ jā saktā hũ?
  - मैं India क्यों नहीं जा सकता हूँ ?

- Why are they wasting time?
  - Ve samay kyõ kharāb kar rahe haĩ?
  - वे समय क्यों खराब कर रहे हैं ?

- Why is the Earth round?
  - Pruthvī (Earth) gol kyõ hai?
  - पृथ्वी गोल क्यों है ?

- Why did you do this?
- Āpne aisā kyō kiyā?
- आपने ऐसा क्यों किया ?

(kiyā is used in the past indefinite form of karnā)

- Why am I tired?
- Maĩ thakā kyō hū̃?
- मैं थका क्यों हूँ ?

Exercise 12.7 Help Pingu translate the following sentences into Hindi.

1. Why is the sky blue?
2. Why are you learning Hindi?
3. Why can't she answer?
4. Why is my belly hurting?
5. Why are they not coming to our house?

Watch the video "Hindi Interrogative -1" and "Hindi Interrogative -2" at YouTube.com/HindiUniversity to deepen your learning.

Hindi Vocabulary

English	Hindi	Devanagari
Point	Matlab	मतलब
Goal	Maksad	मकसद
Aim	Lakshya	लक्ष्य
View	Mat	मत
Favorite sport	Pasādīdā khel	पसंदीदा खेल
School	Vidhyālay	विद्यालय
Passport	Abhay Patr	अभय पत्र
Office	Daftar	दफ़्तर
Qualification	Yogyatā	योग्यता
Strength	Tāqat	ताक़त
Weakness	Kamzorī	कमज़ोरी
Age	Umr	उम्र
Vacation	Chhuttī	छुट्टी
Wedding	Shādī	शादी
Key	Chābī	चाबी
Ceremony	Rīti	रीति
Health	Tabiyat	तबियत
Tonight	Āj rāt	आज रात
To stay	Thaharnā	ठहरना
To drive	Chalānā	चलाना

Conversation Between Mara and Nora

Mara: Namaste Nora, Tum kaisī ho?
नमस्ते Nora, तुम कैसी हो ?

Nora: Namaste Mara, Maĩ thīk hū̃. Aur tum? Tumhārī nayī naukrī kaisī hai?
नमस्ते Mara, मैं ठीक हूँ ! और तुम ? तुम्हारी नयी नौकरी कैसी है ?

Mara: Thodī mushkil hai.
थोड़ी मुश्किल है ।

Nora: Kyō̃?
क्यों ?

Mara: Sab kuch nayā hai aur maĩ abhī akelī rehtī hū̃.
सब कुछ नया है और मैं अभी अकेली रहती हूँ ।

Nora: Tumhārā ghar kahā̃ hai? Tumhāre daftar ke pās?
तुम्हारा घर कहाँ है ? तुम्हारे दफ्तर के पास ?

Mara: Hā̃, shehar mẽ. Tum kab ā rahī ho?
हाँ, शहर में । तुम कब आ रही हो ?

Nora: Maĩ agle saptāh Ady ke sāth āū̃gī.
मैं अगले सप्ताह Ady के साथ आऊँगी ।

Mara: Ady kaun hai? Tumhārā nayā dost?
Ady कौन है ? तुम्हारा नया दोस्त ?

Nora: Hā̃. Vah bahut achhā ādmī hai.
हाँ । वह बहुत अच्छा आदमी है ।

Mara: Bahut achchhā, Apnā dhyān rakhnā.
बहुत अच्छा, अपना ध्यान रखना ।

Nora: Shukriyā, Tum bhī.
शुक्रिया, तुम भी ।

Conversation Between Ady and Nora

Ady: Namaste Nora, Āp kaisī haĩ?
नमस्ते Nora , आप कैसी हैं ?

Nora: Namaste Ady, Maĩ thīk hũ, shukriya, Aur āp kaise haĩ? Kahā̃ jā rahe haĩ?
नमस्ते Ady , मैं ठीक हूँ , शुक्रिया , और आप कैसे हैं ? कहाँ जा रहे हैं ?

Ady: Maĩ thīk nahī̃ hũ. Maĩ mere bete ke vidhyālay jā rahā hũ.
मैं ठीक नहीं हूँ । मैं मेरे बेटे के विद्यालय जा रहा हूँ ।

Nora: Kyõ? Kyā bāt hai? Kaun sā betā, Charlie?
क्यों ? क्या बात है ? कौन सा बेटा , Charlie ?

Ady: Nahī̃ nahī̃, Peter. Vah uskī kitāb ghar mẽ bhul gayā. Maĩ nārāz hũ kyõ kī vah roz kuch bhultā hai.
नहीं नहीं , Peter । वह उसकी किताब घर में भूल गया । मैं नाराज़ हूँ क्यों कि वह रोज़ कुछ भूलता है ।

Nora: Mujhe lagtā hai ki āpko nahī̃ jānā chāhiye.
मुझे लगता है कि आपको नहीं जाना चाहिए ।

Ady: To vah nahī̃ padhegā!
तो वह नहीं पढ़ेगा !

Chapter 13

Pingu is beautiful

PINGU IS AMAZED BY THE BEAUTIFUL SOUTHERN LIGHTS

+ Pingu will learn to describe herself in Hindi.

Adjectives

Adjectives are words used to describe a noun or a pronoun (i.e., big boy, tall girl, small car, etc.). There are two types of adjectives in Hindi: Inflected and uninflected. By the end of this chapter, you will learn to use Hindi adjectives and make sentences such as the following:

- Tall girl
- Small house
- Yellow shirt

Case 1: Inflected adjectives

If the adjective changes based on the gender of the noun (i.e., masculine/ feminine) or based on the number (singular vs. plural), it's an "inflected adjective".

"Big" in Hindi is known as "Badā". "Badā" is considered an inflected adjective in Hindi. In English, the word "big" doesn't change in any of the following sentences.

- Big boy / Big boys
- Big girl / Big girls

In Hindi, the adjective "badā" changes based on the noun it is used with. Review the scenarios below.

English	Hindi	Explanation
Big boy	Badā ladkā बड़ा लड़का	There is an "ā" sound at the end of the adjective when using it with masculine singular nouns.
Big boys	Bade ladke बड़े लड़के	There is an "e" sound at the end of the adjective when using it with masculine plural nouns.
Big girl	Badī ladkī बड़ी लड़की	There is an "ī" sound at the end of the adjective when using it with feminine singular nouns.
Big girls	Badī ladkiyā̃ बड़ी लड़कियाँ	There is an "ī" sound at the end of the adjective when using it with feminine plural nouns.

Example 1:

Given the above table, can you translate the following sentences into English?

Hint: Small = Chhotā छोटा (masculine singular)

- Small boy / Small boys
- Small girl / Small girls

Since it's a newer concept, I will provide the answers here:

- Small boy
- Chhotā ladkā
- छोटा लड़का

- Small boys
- Chhote ladke
- छोटे लड़के

- Small car
- Chhotī ladkī
- छोटी लड़की

- Small cars
- Chhotī ladkiyā̃
- छोटी लड़कियाँ

Example 2:

Let's do another example.

room = kamrā कमरा (masculine), car = gādī गाड़ी (feminine)

- Big room
- Badā kamrā
- बड़ा कमरा

- Big rooms
- Bade kamre
- बड़े कमरे

- Big car
- Badī gādī
- बड़ी गाड़ी

- Big cars
- Badī gādiyā̃
- बड़ी गाड़ियाँ

Case 2: Uninflected adjectives

If the adjective does not change based on the gender of the noun (i.e., masculine /feminine) or based on the number (singular vs. plural), it's an "uninflected adjective".

Example: sundar सुंदर = beautiful

English	Hindi	Explanation
Beautiful boy	Sundar ladkā सुंदर लड़का	You will notice that the adjective does not change in all the scenarios.
Beautiful boys	Sundar ladke सुंदर लड़के	
Beautiful girl	Sundar ladkī सुंदर लड़की	
Beautiful girls	Sundar ladkiyā̃ सुंदर लड़कियाँ	

Another example: Safed सफ़ेद = White

English	Hindi	Explanation
White cloth	Safed kapdā सफ़ेद कपड़ा	You will notice that the adjective does not change in all the scenarios.
White clothes	Safed kapde सफ़ेद कपड़े	
White Car	Safed gādī सफ़ेद गाड़ी	
White Cars	Safed gādiyā̃ सफ़ेद गाड़ियाँ	

Exercise 13.1 Help Pingu fill in the table with the correct adjective form.

Adjectives	Kursī	Jūte	Ghar	Kitābē
Purānā	Purānī kursī			
Sundar				
Ākhirī				
Gandā				

> Watch the video "Hindi Adjectives" at YouTube.com/HindiUniversity (playlist: Pingu Learns To Speak Hindi) to deepen your learning.

Case 3: Using post-positions with adjectives

Now that you have learned about inflected/uninflected adjectives, I want to discuss how to use post-positions with these adjectives. What happens when you want to make sentences like the following:

- Big boy's laptop (masculine singular)
- Big boys' laptop (masculine plural)
- Big girl's laptop (feminine singular)
- Big girls' laptop (feminine plural)

You will notice that both "badā" and "ladkā" change form to an oblique case. The oblique case is an essential concept in Hindi, where Hindi nouns, pronouns, and adjectives

change when followed by postpositions. See the table below:

Big boy	Big boy's	Big Boy's laptop	Explanation
Badā ladkā बड़ा लड़का	Badā ladkā + kā बड़ा लड़का + का	Bade ladke kā laptop बड़े लड़के का laptop	You will notice that both "badā" and "ladkā" change form to an oblique case.

Big boys	Big boys'	Big boys' laptop	Explanation
Bade ladke बड़े लड़के	Bade ladke + kā बड़े लड़के + का	Bade ladkõ kā laptop बड़े लड़कों का laptop	You will notice that only the noun "ladke" changes form to an oblique case (ladkõ).

Big girl	Big girl's	Big girl's laptop	Explanation
Badī ladkī बड़ी लड़की	Badī ladkī + kā बड़ी लड़की + का	Badī ladkī kā laptop बड़ी लड़की का laptop	You will notice that neither "badī" nor "ladkī" change form.

Big girls	Big girls'	Big girls' laptop	Explanation
Badī ladkiyā̃ बड़ी लड़कियाँ	Badī Ladkiyā̃ + kā बड़ी लड़कियाँ + का	Badī Ladkiyõ kā laptop बड़ी लड़कियाँ का laptop	You will notice that only the noun "ladkiyā̃" changes form to an oblique case (ladkiyõ).

Exercise 13.2 Given the above example, can you help Pingu translate the following sentences into Hindi?

- masculine singular
- feminine singular

1 Small boy's brother _____
2 Small boys' brother _____
3 Small girl's brother _____
4 Small girls' brother _____

Since it's a newer concept, I will provide some hints here:

Small boy's

- chhotā ladkā + kā → chhote ladke kā
- छोटा लड़का + का → छोटे लड़के का

Small boys'

- chhote ladke + kā → chhote ladkõ kā
- छोटे लड़के + का → छोटे लड़कों का

Small girl's

- chhotī ladkī + kā → chhotī ladkī kā
- छोटी लड़की + का → छोटी लड़की का

Small girls'

- chhotī ladkiyā̃ → chhotī ladkiyõ kā
- छोटी लड़कियाँ + का → छोटी लड़कियों का

Case 4: Making advanced sentences using adjectives

Let's try to make some advanced sentences based on what we have learned so far. Consider that you want to make sentences like the following:

- I walk in front of a big boy.
- I walk in front of big boys.
- I walk in front of a big girl.
- I walk in front of big girls.

You will notice the above sentences have a combination of the simple present tense (i.e., I walk), a compound postposition (in front of), an adjective, and a noun (big boy(s)/girl(s)).

Let's break it down into three parts:

Part 1	I walk.	Maĩ chaltā hũ.	मैं चलता हूँ ।
Part 2	In front of	Ke āge	के आगे
Part 3	Big boy	Badā ladkā	बड़ा लड़का
	Big boys	Bade ladke	बड़े लड़के
	Big girl	Bbadī ladkī	बड़ी लड़की
	Big girls	Badī ladkiyā̃	बड़ी लड़कियाँ

Your goal is to combine part 1, 2, and 3, so that verb conjugation makes sense:

- I walk in front of a big boy.
- I walk in front of big boys.
- I walk in front of a big girl.
- I walk in front of big girls.

- Maĩ bade ladke ke āge chaltā hũ.
- मैं बड़े लड़के के आगे चलता हूँ ।

- Maĩ bade ladkõ ke āge chaltā hũ.
- मैं बड़े लड़कों के आगे चलता हूँ ।

- Maĩ badī ladkī ke āge chaltā hũ.
- मैं बड़ी लड़की के आगे चलता हूँ ।

- Maĩ badī ladkiyõ ke āge chaltā hũ.
- मैं बड़ी लड़कियों के आगे चलता हूँ ।

Let's try changing the pronouns:

- You walk in front of a big boy.
- We walk in front of big boys.

- Āp bade ladke ke āge chalte haĩ.
- आप बड़े लड़के के आगे चलते हैं ।

- Hum bade ladkõ ke āge chalte haĩ.
- हम बड़े लड़कों के आगे चलते हैं ।

- They walk in front of a big girl.
- He walks in front of big girls.

- Ve badī ladkī ke āge chalte haĩ.
- वे बड़ी लड़की के आगे चलते हैं ।

- Vah badī ladkiyõ ke āge chaltā hai.
- वह बड़ी लड़कियों के आगे चलता है ।

Exercise 13.3 Help Pingu translate the following sentences to Hindi.

1. They were walking in front of the car.
2. She was driving a white car.
3. He is buying a yellow flower.
4. We are swimming in the blue river.
5. Sarah is not eating hot curry.
6. Is she buying a new sari from India?

Hindi Vocabulary

Colors		
English	**Hindi**	**Devanagari**
White	Safed	सफेद
Black	Kālā	काला
Yellow	Pīlā	पीला
Blue	Nīlā	नीला
Green	Harā	हरा
Red	Lāl	लाल
Brown	Bhūrā	भूरा
Orange	Nārangī	नारंगी

Inflected Adjectives		
English	Hindi	Devanagari
Big	Badā	बड़ा
Few	Thodā	थोड़ा
Good	Acchā	अच्छा
High	Ũchā	ऊँचा
Little	Chhotā	छोटा
Long	Lambā	लंबा
New	Nayā	नया
Old	Purānā	पुराना
Next	Aglā	अगला
First	Pehlā	पहला
Other	Dūsrā	दूसरा
Thirsty	Pyāsā	प्यासा
Hungry	Bhūkhā	भूखा
Bad	Burā	बुरा
Old (age)	Būdhā	बूढ़ा
Dirty	Gandā	गंदा
Wet	Gīlā	गीला
Dry	Sūkhā	सूखा
Thin	Patlā	पतला
Fat	Motā	मोटा

UnInflected Adjectives		
English	Hindi	Devanagari
Bad	Kharāb	खराब
Different	Alag	अलग
Early	Jaldī	जल्दी
Great	Mahān	महान
Last	Ākhirī	आखिरी
Right	Sahī	सही
Same	Samān	समान
Young	Jawān	जवान
Beautiful	Sundar	सुंदर
Sad	Dukhī	दुःखी
Happy	Khush	खुश
Clean	Sāf	साफ
Easy	Āsān	आसान
Difficult	Mushkil	मुश्किल
Hard	Kathin	कठिन
Wrong	Galat	गलत
Lazy	Ālsī	आलसी
Honest	Īmāndār	ईमानदार
Kind	Dayālu	दयालु
Mad	Pāgal	पागल

Get inspired by HindiUniversity students

Nora (Norwey)

Merā nām Nora hai aur āj āpko maĩ apne shehar ke bāre mẽ batāũgī. Vah kuch bade pahādõ ke pās hai. Vah chotā hai lekin bahut sundar aur bahut sāf hai. Uske rāste tang haĩ par yahā̃ gādiyā̃ bahut kam haĩ. Dukānõ ke bāhar rangīn phūl haĩ. Hum har din dukānõ mẽ tāze phal kharīdte haĩ. Yahā̃ log khush aur swasth hai. Kripayā mere shehar mẽ āiye!

मेरा नाम Nora है और आज आपको मैं अपने शहर के बारे में बताऊँगी। वह कुछ बड़े पहाड़ों के पास है। वह छोटा है लेकिन बहुत सुंदर और बहुत साफ है। उसके रास्ते तंग हैं पर यहाँ गाड़ियाँ बहुत कम हैं। दुकानों के बाहर रंगीन फूल हैं। हम हर दिन दुकानों में ताज़े फल खरीदते है। यहाँ लोग खुश और स्वस्थ है। कृपया मेरे शहर में आइए !

Mara (Norwey)

Merā nām Mara hai. Mere do bacche haĩ. Hum ek chote gā̃v mẽ rehte haĩ. Humāre ghar ke pīche ek lambī nadī hai aur nadī ke pās ek badā jangal hai. Jangal ke andar bahut sundar ped haĩ aur alag alag jānvar haĩ. Har din ped ke ūpar rangīn pakshī āte haĩ. Maĩ sochtī hũ ki yah jagah mahān hai !

मेरा नाम Mara है । मेरे दो बच्चे हैं । हम एक छोटे गाँव में रहते हैं । हमारे घर के पीछे एक लंबी नदी है और नदी के पास एक बड़ा जंगल है । जंगल के अंदर बहुत सुंदर पेड़ हैं और अलग अलग जानवर हैं । हर दिन पेड़ के ऊपर रंगीन पक्षी आते हैं । मैं सोचती हूँ कि यह जगह महान है !

Tara (Iran)

Mere chote kamre mẽ dīvār ke pās merā bistar hai. Bistar ke nīche ek lakdī kā box hai. Box ke andar tīn pyārī guriyā̃, ek sundar bag, ek nayā jūtā, do chotī aur lāl gāriyā̃, rangīn pencil aur chār purāntī bacchõ kī kitābẽ haĩ. Maĩ ab badī hũ lekin ye mere bachpan kī mīthī yādẽ haĩ.

मेरे छोटे कमरे में दीवार के पास मेरा बिस्तर है । बिस्तर के नीचे एक लकड़ी का box है । Box के अंदर तीन प्यारी गुड़ियाँ , एक सुंदर bag, एक नया जूता , दो छोटी गाड़ियाँ , रंगीन pencil और चार पुरानी बच्चों की किताबें हैं । मैं अब बड़ी हूँ लेकिन ये मेरे बचपन की मीठी यादें हैं ।

Chapter 14

Pingu was walking slowly

Pingu is a quick swimmer...

† Pingu will learn to talk about the Hindi learning experience, how long it took her, when she began learning, where did she learn, and many more adventures.

Adverbs

In this chapter, we will learn about Hindi Adverbs. Adverbs are the words that describe "how", "when", "where" and "to what extent" in a given sentence. You have learned to say several Hindi sentences by now. However, if you want to form more complex sentences, then Hindi adverbs are your best friends.

By the end of this chapter, you will learn to use Hindi adverbs and make sentences such as the following:

- She was playing carefully.
- He entered the house quietly.
- I recently watched this movie.
- We didn't see anything.
- You are extremely beautiful.
- They were very sick last week.

Alright, are you ready? Let's get started. We will be covering adverbs in four sections.

- Adverbs that answer the "*how*" questions.
- Adverbs that answer the "*when*" questions.
- Adverbs that answer the "*where*" questions.
- Adverbs that answer the "*to what extent*" questions.

Adverbs that answer "How"

English	Hindi	Devanagari
Carefully	Dhyān se	ध्यान से
Quickly	Jaldī se	जल्दी से
Quietly	Dhīre se	धीरे से
Loudly	Zor se	ज़ोर से
Easily	Āsānī se	आसानी से
Fluently	Dhadalle se	धड़ल्ले से

I encourage you to first focus on the limited set of adverbs, master them, and then continue to learn more.

Now, let's see some examples with and without the adverbs:

- They were playing.
- Ve khel rahe the.
- वे खेल रहे थे ।

- They were playing carefully.
- Ve dhyān se khel rahe the.
- वे ध्यान से खेल रहे थे ।

- She was walking.
- Vah chal rahī thī.
- वह चल रही थी ।

- She was walking slowly.
- Vah dhīre se chal rahī thī.
- वह धीरे से चल रही थी ।

- She was talking.
- Vah bol rahī thī.
- वह बोल रही थी ।

- She was talking loudly.
- Vah zor se bol rahī thī.
- वह ज़ोर से बोल रही थी ।

Exercise 14.1 Help Pingu complete the following sentences.

1 Usne ___ game jītā. (easily)
2 Unhõne ___ 911 call kiyā. (quickly)
3 Maĩ ___ hāsā. (loudly)
4 Āpne ___ traffic mẽ gāḍī calāyī. (carefully)

१ उसने ___ game जीता ।
२ उन्होंने ___ 911 call किया ।
३ मैं ___ हँसा ।
४ आपने ___ traffic में गाड़ी चलायी ।

Exercise 14.2 Help Pingu translate the following sentences into Hindi.

1 I laughed loudly in school.
2 They spoke quietly at the restaurant.
3 We spoke fluently in French.
4 You swam lazily in the pool.
5 They met secretly at the temple.
6 She sat happily in the house.

Exercise 14.3 Help Pingu translate the following sentences into Hindi.

1. Did you laugh loudly in school?
2. They didn't speak quietly at the restaurant.
3. Did she speak fluently in French?
4. Did you swim lazily in the pool?
5. Didn't they meet secretly in the temple?
6. She didn't sit in the house happily.

Adverbs that answer "When"

English	Hindi	Devanagari
Recently	Hāl hī mẽ	हाल ही में
Right now	Abhī	अभी
Soon	Jaldī / Jaldī hī	जल्दी / जल्दी ही
Later	Bād mẽ	बाद में
Still	Abhī tak	अभी तक
Earlier	Pehle	पहले

- I went to New York.
  - Maĩ New York gayā.
  - मैं New York गया ।

- I went to New York recently.
  - Maĩ hāl hī mẽ New York gayā.
  - मैं हाल ही में New York गया ।

- I am eating a dosa.
  - Maĩ dosā khā rahā hū̃.
  - मैं डोसा खा रहा हूँ ।

- I am eating a dosa right now.
  - Maĩ abhī dosā khā rahā hū̃.
  - मैं अभी डोसा खा रहा हूँ ।

- I am busy.
- I am busy right now.
- I will come to your house soon.
- I will come to your house later.
- I am still fixing it.

- Maĩ vyast hũ.
- मैं व्यस्त हूँ ।
- Maĩ abhī vyast hũ.
- मैं अभी व्यस्त हूँ ।
- Maĩ āpke ghar jaldī hī āũgā.
- मैं आपके घर जल्दी ही आऊँगा ।
- Maĩ āpke ghar bād mẽ āũgā.
- मैं आपके घर बाद में आऊँगा ।
- Maĩ abhī tak ise thīk kar rahā hũ.
- मैं अभी तक इसे ठीक कर रहा हूँ ।

Adverbs that answer "Where"

English	Hindi	Devanagari
Here	Yahã	यहाँ
There	Vahã	वहाँ
Everywhere	Har jagah	हर जगह
Anywhere	Kahĩ bhī	कहीं भी
Nowhere	Kahĩ nahĩ	कहीं नहीं
Inside	Andar	अंदर
Outside	Bāhar	बाहर

- They were playing.
- They were playing here.

- Ve khel rahe the.
- वे खेल रहे थे ।
- Ve yahã khel rahe the.
- वे यहाँ खेल रहे थे ।

- Right now, you can't travel.
- Right now, you can't travel anywhere.

- Abhī āp ghūm nahī̃ sakte hai.
- अभी आप घूम नहीं सकते है।
- Abhī āp kahī̃ nahī̃ ghūm sakte hai.
- अभी आप कहीं नहीं घूम सकते है।

Adverbs that answer "To what extent"

English	Hindi	Devanagari
Quite	Bahut	बहुत
Very	Bahut / Bahut hī	बहुत / बहुत ही
Extremely	Bahut zyādā	बहुत ज़्यादा
Really	Sahi mẽ / Vāstav mẽ	सही में / वास्तव में
Little bit	Thodā	थोड़ा

- This is expensive.
  - Yah mahãgā hai.
  - यह महँगा है।

- This is very expensive.
  - Yah bahut mahãgā hai.
  - यह बहुत महँगा है।

- This is cheap.
  - Yah sastā hai.
  - यह सस्ता है।

- This is very cheap.
  - Yah bahut sastā hai.
  - यह बहुत सस्ता है।

- This is clean.
  - Yah sāf hai.
  - यह साफ़ है।

- It's quite clean.
  - Yah kāfī sāf hai.
  - यह काफी साफ़ है।

Exercise 14.4 Help Pingu translate the following sentences into Hindi.

1 He recently wrote a book.
2 I will see my brother later.
3 What are you doing right now?
4 Are they still eating?
5 We were not watching a movie earlier.
6 She will start her new job soon.

Exercise 14.5 Help Pingu fill in the blanks with the correct adverb and translate the sentences.

> thoḍā   har jagah   bahut   kahī̃ bhī   vāstav   kahī̃ nahī̃

1 Yah gānā _____ mẽ acchā hai.
2 Āp uskī kitāb _____ kharīd sakte haĩ.
3 Hum uske bāre mẽ _____ pareshān hote haĩ.
4 Vah is sāl _____ nahī̃ jā rahī hai.
5 Ve bahut _____ khush haĩ kyõ ki unhõne ek nayā ghar kharīdā.
6 Maĩ is saptāh _____ jānā chāhtī hū̃.

१ यह गाना _____ में अच्छा है ।
२ आप उसकी किताब _____ ख़रीद सकते हैं ।
३ हम उसके बारे में _____ परेशान होते हैं ।
४ वह इस साल _____ नहीं जा रही है ।
५ वे _____ ख़ुश हैं क्यों कि उन्होंने एक नया घर ख़रीदा ।
६ मैं इस सप्ताह _____ जाना चाहती हूँ ।

Watch the video "Hindi Adverbs" at YouTube.com/HindiUniversity (playlist: Pingu Learns To Speak Hindi) to deepen your learning.

Language learning Patterns

In this section, you will see a quick summary of how a complex Hindi sentence can be simplified using 7 steps:

Example:

- Sometimes I eat a red apple with my food for lunch.
- Maĩ kabhī kabhī lunch pe khāne ke sāth lāl seb khātā hũ.
- मैं कभी कभी lunch पे खाने के साथ लाल सेब खाता हूँ।

Step 1	Find the verb	khānā = to eat	
Step 2	Find the tense	present simple	I eat (Maĩ khātā hũ)
Step 3	Find the object	seb = apple	I eat an apple (Maĩ seb khātā hũ)
Step 4	Identify if there an adjective	lāl = red	I eat a red apple (Maĩ lāl seb khātā hũ)
Step 5	Identify if there an adverb	kabhī kabhī = sometimes	Sometimes, I eat a red apple (Maĩ kabhī kabhī lāl seb khātā hũ)
Step 6	Identify if there a post-position	pe = for	Sometimes, I eat a red apple for lunch (Maĩ kabhī kabhī lunch pe lāl seb khātā hũ)
Step 7	making it complex	khāne ke sāth = with my food	Sometimes, I eat a red apple with my food for lunch (Maĩ kabhī kabhī lunch pe khāne ke sāth lāl seb khātā hũ)

Watch the video "Hindi Language Patterns" to deepen your learning.

Get inspired by HindiUniversity students

Lia (Spain)

Merā nām Lia hai. Maĩ hāl hī mẽ apnī bahan ke ghar gayī. Uskā shehar bahut zyādā sundar hai aur uskā ghar bahut hī baḍā hai. Uske tīn bacche haĩ. Har jagah khilaune haĩ. Bacche ghar ke andar zor se bolte haĩ aur ve jaldī se dauḍte haĩ. Maĩ abhī tak unkī āvāz ko sun rahī hũ. Maĩ unke sāth bahut hãsī. Abhī mujhko dūsrī chuttī chāhiye!

मेरा नाम Lia है. मैं हाल ही में अपनी बहन के घर गयी. उसका शहर बहुत ज़्यादा सुंदर है और उसका घर बहुत ही बड़ा है. उसके तीन बच्चे हैं। हर जगह खिलौने हैं. बच्चे घर के अंदर ज़ोर से बोलते हैं और वे जल्दी से दौड़ते हैं. मैं अभी तक उनकी आवाज़ को सुन रही हूँ. मैं उनके साथ बहुत हँसी. अभी मुझको दूसरी छुट्टी चाहिए !

Ananya (USA)

Merā nām Ananya hai aur maĩ patrakār hũ. Maĩ ek chote shehar mẽ rehtī hũ. Maĩ har jagah ghūmtī hũ. Maĩ hāl hī mẽ India gayī. India vāstav mẽ ek sundar desh hai. Maĩ abhī Australia mẽ hũ. Maĩ merā kām jaldī se karūgī aur maĩ jaldī hī Italy vāpas jāũgī. Merī ek laḍkī hai aur mujhko chhuttī chāhiye !

मेरा नाम Ananya है और मैं पत्रकार हूँ । मैं एक छोटे शहर में रहती हूँ । मैं हर जगह घूमती हूँ। मैं हाल ही में India गयी । India वास्तव में एक सुंदर देश है। मैं अभी Australia में हूँ। मैं मेरा काम जल्दी से करूँगी और मैं जल्दी ही Italy वापस जाऊँगी । मेरी एक लड़की है और मुझको छुट्टी चाहिए !

Answer Sheet

CHAPTER 1

Exercise 1.1

Merā nām Pingu hai. Maĩ Antarctica se hū̃.
मेरा नाम Pingu है । मैं Antarctica से हूँ ।

Exercise 1.2

Maĩ Hindī learner hū̃. (written for Penguin) मैं हिन्दी learner हूँ ।

Exercise 1.3

Maĩ Antarctica se hū̃. (written for Penguin) मैं Antarctica से हूँ ।

Exercise 1.4

1. Maĩ philosopher hū̃.   १ मैं philosopher हूँ ।
2. Maĩ coin collector hū̃.   २ मैं coin collector हूँ ।
3. Maĩ diabetic hū̃.   ३ मैं diabetic हूँ ।
4. Maĩ christian hū̃.   ४ मैं christian हूँ ।

Exercise 1.5

1. Maĩ bhāī hū̃.   १ मैं भाई हूँ ।
2. Maĩ dādā jī hū̃.   २ मैं दादा जी हूँ ।
3. Maĩ bacchī hū̃.   ३ मैं बच्ची हूँ ।

Exercise 1.6

It's okay to use the English word here; remember you just started learning the Hindi language.

1. Maĩ nervous hũ.
2. Maĩ calm hũ.
3. Maĩ angry hũ.
4. Maĩ excited hũ.

१ मैं nervous हूँ ।
२ मैं calm हूँ ।
३ मैं angry हूँ ।
४ मैं excited हूँ ।

Exercise 1.7

1. Maĩ old hũ.
2. Maĩ young hũ.
3. Maĩ strong hũ.

१ मैं old हूँ ।
२ मैं young हूँ ।
३ मैं strong हूँ ।

Exercise 1.8

1. Maĩ active hũ.
2. Maĩ involved hũ.
3. Maĩ knowledgeable hũ.

१ मैं active हूँ ।
२ मैं involved हूँ ।
३ मैं knowledgeable हूँ ।

Exercise 1.9

1. Maĩ India se hũ.
2. Maĩ Taiwan se hũ

१ मैं India से हूँ ।
२ मैं Taiwan से हूँ ।

Exercise 1.10

1. Maĩ Nepal mẽ hũ.
2. Maĩ school mẽ hũ.

१ मैं Nepal में हूँ ।
२ मैं school में हूँ ।

Exercise 1.11

1. Hindī mẽ <u>mountain</u> ko <u>pahād</u> kehte hai.
2. Hindī mẽ <u>friend</u> ko <u>dost</u> kehte hai.

१ हिन्दी में <u>mountain</u> को <u>पहाड़</u> कहते है ।
२ हिन्दी में <u>friend</u> को <u>दोस्त</u> कहते है ।

CHAPTER 2

Exercise 2.1

Feminine chittī (चिट्ठी), bhūkh (भूख), ā̃kh (आँख), nānī (नानी), Gãgā (गँगा), gudiyā (गुड़िया), sabjī (सब्ज़ी), Spanish, rāt (रात), sajāwat (सजावट)

Masculine: tel (तेल), bachpan (बचपन), darwāzā (दरवाज़ा), hāth (हाथ), betā (बेटा), gehū̃ (गेहू̃), lagāv (लगाव), lohā (लोहा), Hind mahāsāgar (हिन्द महासागर), hīrā (हीरा), Himālaya (हिमालय)

CHAPTER 3

Exercise 3.1

1	Chehre	१	चेहरे
2	Māthe	२	माथे
3	Tope	३	टोपे
4	Lote	४	लोटे

Exercise 3.2

1	Phone	१	फ़ोन
2	Bāl	२	बाल
3	Hāth	३	हाथ
4	Kāgaz	४	कागज़

Exercise 3.3

1. Deviyā̃ — १ देवियाँ
2. Dawāiyā̃ — २ दवाइयाँ
3. Rajāiyā̃ — ३ रजाइयाँ
4. Kadāhiyā̃ — ४ कड़ाहियाँ

Exercise 3.4

1. Bahanẽ — १ बहिनें
2. Ā̃khẽ — २ आँखें
3. Bātẽ — ३ बातें
4. Mezẽ — ४ मेजें

Exercise 3.5

1. Shīshī - Shīshiyā̃ (feminine) — १ शीशी - शीशियाँ
2. Jūtā - Jūte (masculine) — २ जूता - जूते
3. Palang - Palang (masculine) — ३ पलंग - पलंग
4. Khidkī - Khidkiyā̃ (feminine) — ४ खिड़की - खिड़कियाँ

Exercise 3.6

1. Bob kā lunch — १ Bob का lunch
2. Alicia kā coat — २ Alicia का coat
3. Mia kā pati (Pati - Husband) — ३ Mia का पति
4. Sam kā pen — ४ Sam का pen

Exercise 3.7

1. Pingu ke mātā pitā — १ Pingu के माता पिता
2. Alicia ke coat — २ Alicia के coat
3. Mia ke kapde (kapde = clothes) — ३ Mia के कपड़े
4. Sam ke jūte — ४ Sam के जूते

Exercise 3.8

1. Bob kī pareshāniyā̃. (problem = pareshānī, problems = pareshāniyā̃)
2. Alicia kī sāriyā̃.
3. Mia kī kamzoriyā̃. (kamzorī = weakness, kamzoriyā̃ = weaknesses)

१ Bob की परेशानियाँ । (परेशानी, परेशानियाँ)
२ Alicia की साड़ियाँ ।
३ Mia की कमज़ोरियाँ । (कमज़ोरी, कमज़ोरियाँ)

CHAPTER 4

Exercise 4.1

1	Maĩ khush hū̃.	I am happy.	१ मैं ख़ुश हूँ ।
2	Āp Kahā̃ haĩ?	Where are you?	२ आप कहाँ हैं ?
3	Hum french haĩ.	We are French.	३ हम french हैं ।
4	Vah engineer hai.	He is an engineer.	४ वह engineer है ।
5	Ve bacche haĩ.	They are children.	५ वे बच्चे हैं ।

Exercise 4.2

1	Maĩ yātrī hū̃.	१ मैं यात्री हूँ ।
2	Vah American hai.	२ वह American है ।
3	Hum scientists haĩ.	३ हम scientists हैं ।
4	Ve vegetarian haĩ.	४ वे vegetarian हैं ।
5	Āp amazing haĩ.	५ आप amazing हैं ।
6	Vah tall (lambā) hai.	६ वह tall (लंबा) है ।
7	Vah upset (dukhī) hai.	७ वह upset (दुःखी) है ।

Exercise 4.3

1	Ve nārāz hai.	They are upset.	१ वे नाराज़ है ।
2	Vah kalākār hai.	He is an artist.	२ वह कलाकार है ।
3	Hum pareshān hai.	We are upset.	३ हम परेशान हैं ।

4	Maĩ Lisa hū̃.	I am Lisa.	४ मैं Lisa हूँ ।
5	Āp patrakār haĩ.	You are a journalist.	५ आप पत्रकार हैं ।

Exercise 4.4

I am a songwriter. I am from Italy, but I live in Ireland. I write songs for movies, and I travel a lot to America. I also play the piano and write stories for children.

Maĩ ek gītkār hū̃. Maĩ Italy se hū̃, lekin maĩ Ireland mē rehtā hū̃. Maĩ filmõ ke liye gīt likhtā hū̃ aur maĩ America bahut jātā hū̃. Maĩ piano bhī bajātā hū̃ aur maĩ bacchõ ke liye kahāniyā̃ likhtā hū̃.

मैं एक गीतकार हूँ । मैं Italy से हूँ लेकिन मैं Ireland में रहता हूँ । मैं फिल्मों के लिए गीत लिखता हूँ और मैं America बहुत जाता हूँ । मैं piano भी बजाता हूँ और मैं बच्चों के लिए कहानियाँ लिखता हूँ ।

Exercise 4.5

1	Yah ek ghadī hai.	१ यह एक घड़ी है ।
2	Ve topiyā̃ haĩ.	२ वे टोपियाँ हैं ।
3	Ye mere dost haĩ.	३ ये मेरे दोस्त हैं ।
4	Vah merā patā hai.	४ वह मेरा पता है ।

Exercise 4.6

1 Yah merī bhāshā hai.
   This is my language. / Este es mi idioma.   १ यह मेरी भाषा है ।

2 Vah merā bhāī hai.
   That is my brother. / Ese es mi hermano.   २ वह मेरा भाई है ।

3 Ye kapde haĩ.
   These are clothes. / Esto es ropa.   ३ ये कपड़े हैं ।

4 Ve vidhyārtī haĩ.
   Those are students. / Esos son universitarios.   ४ वे विद्यार्थी हैं ।

Exercise 4.7

1. Yah humārā ghar hai.
2. Vah merā bhāī hai.
3. Vah merī bahan hai.
4. Ye uske dost haĩ.
5. Vah āpke adhyāpk hai.
6. Unkī gādī badī haĩ.
7. Yah tumhārī kitāb hai.
8. Uskā kamrā chotā hai.
9. Merī betī vivāhit hai.
10. Āpka betā swasth hai.

१ यह हमारा घर है ।
२ वह मेरा भाई है ।
३ वह मेरी बहन है ।
४ ये उसके दोस्त है ।
५ वह आपके अध्यापक है ।
६ उनकी गाड़ी बड़ी हैं ।
७ यह तुम्हारी किताब है ।
८ उसका कमरा छोटा है ।
९ मेरी बेटी विवाहित है ।
१० आपका बेटा स्वस्थ है ।

CHAPTER 5

Exercise 5.1

1. Hum Pizza khāte haĩ.
2. Vah gānā gāti hai.
3. Āp TV dekhte haĩ.
4. Tum kītāb padhte ho.
5. Maĩ pānī pītā hū̃.
6. Ve football khelte haĩ.

१ हम pizza खाते हैं ।
२ वह गाना गाती है ।
३ आप TV देखते हैं ।
४ तुम किताब पढ़ते हो ।
५ मैं पानी पीता हूँ ।
६ वे football खेलते हैं ।

Exercise 5.2

1. Maĩ India mẽ cricket <u>kheltā hū̃</u>.
2. Ve subah chāy <u>pīte haĩ</u>.
3. Hum french <u>bolte haĩ</u>.
4. Āp samay pe <u>sote haĩ</u>.
5. Vah har din bhajan <u>gātā hai</u>.
6. Vah Bollywood films <u>dekhtī hai</u>.

१ मैं India में cricket <u>खेलता हूँ</u> ।
२ वे सुबह चाय <u>पीते हैं</u> ।
३ हम french <u>बोलते हैं</u> ।
४ आप समय पे <u>सोते हैं</u> ।
५ वह हर दिन भजन <u>गाता है</u> ।
६ वह Bollywood films <u>देखती है</u> ।

Exercise 5.3

1. Vah American nahī̃ hai.
2. Hum protesters nahī̃ haĩ.
3. Vah lambā nahī̃ hai.
4. Hum pareshān nahī̃ haĩ.
5. Vah funny nahī̃ hai.

१ वह American नहीं है ।
२ हम protesters नहीं हैं ।
३ वह लंबा नहीं है ।
४ हम परेशान नहीं हैं ।
५ वह funny नहीं है ।

Exercise 5.4

1. Maĩ India mẽ cricket nahī̃ kheltā hū̃.
2. Ve subah chāy nahī̃ pīte haĩ.
3. Hum French nahī̃ bolte haĩ.
4. Āp samay pe nahī̃ sote haĩ.
5. Vah roz bhajan nahī̃ gātā hai.
6. Vah Bollywood movies nahī̃ dekhtī hai.

१ मैं India में cricket नहीं खेलता हूँ ।
२ वे सुबह चाय नहीं पीते हैं ।
३ हम French नहीं बोलते हैं ।
४ आप समय पे नहीं सोते हैं ।
५ वह रोज़ भजन नहीं गाता है ।
६ वह bollywood movies नहीं देखती है ।

Exercise 5.5

1. Kyā vah American hai?
2. Kyā hum lambe haĩ?
3. Kyā vah ek mathematician hai?
4. Kyā maĩ lucky hū̃?
5. Kyā vah funny hai?

१ क्या वह American है ?
२ क्या हम लंबे हैं ?
३ क्या वह एक mathematician है ?
४ क्या मैं lucky हूँ ?
५ क्या वह funny है ?

Exercise 5.6

1. Kyā ve India mẽ cricket khelte haĩ?
2. Kyā āp subah chāy pīte haĩ?
3. Kyā vah French boltā hai?
4. Kyā āp samay pe sote haĩ?
5. Kyā vah roz bhajan gātī hai?
6. Kyā āp Bollywood movies dekhte haĩ?

१ क्या वे India में cricket खेलते हैं ?
२ क्या आप सुबह चाय पीते हैं ?
३ क्या वह French बोलता है ?
४ क्या आप समय पे सोते हैं ?
५ क्या वह रोज़ भजन गाती है ?
६ क्या आप Bollywood movies देखते हैं ?

Exercise 5.7

1. Kyā vah American nahī̃ hai?
2. Kyā hum lambe nahī̃ haĩ?
3. Kyā vah nurs nahī̃ hai?
4. Kyā maĩ lucky nahī̃ hū̃?
5. Kyā vah funny nahī̃ hai?

१. क्या वह American नहीं है ?
२. क्या हम लंबे नहीं हैं ?
३. क्या वह नर्स नहीं है ?
४. क्या मैं lucky नहीं हूँ ?
५. क्या वह funny नहीं है ?

Exercise 5.8

1. Kyā ve India mẽ cricket nahī̃ khelte haĩ?
2. Kyā āp subah chāy nahī̃ pīte haĩ?
3. Kyā vah French nahī̃ boltā hai?
4. Kyā āp samay pe nahī̃ sote haĩ?
5. Kyā vah roz bhajan nahī̃ gātī hai?

१. क्या वे India में cricket नहीं खेलते हैं ?
२. क्या आप सुबह चाय नहीं पीते हैं ?
३. क्या वह French नहीं बोलता है ?
४. क्या आप समय पे नहीं सोते हैं ?
५. क्या वह रोज़ भजन नहीं गाती है ?

CHAPTER 6

Exercise 6.1

1. Maĩ Hindī movie dekh rahā hū̃.
2. Maĩ Hindī movie dekh rahī hū̃.
3. Āp Hindī movie dekh rahe haĩ.
4. Hum Hindī movie dekh rahe haĩ.
5. Ve Hindī movie dekh rahe haĩ.
6. Vah Hindī movie dekh rahā hai.
7. Vah Hindī movie dekh rahī hai.

१. मैं हिन्दी movie देख रहा हूँ ।
२. मैं हिन्दी movie देख रही हूँ ।
३. आप हिन्दी movie देख रहे हैं ।
४. हम हिन्दी movie देख रहे हैं ।
५. वे हिन्दी movie देख रहे हैं ।
६. वह हिन्दी movie देख रहा है ।
७. वह हिन्दी movie देख रही है ।

1. I am watching a Hindi movie.
2. I am watching a Hindi movie.
3. You are watching a Hindi movie.
4. We are watching a Hindi movie.
5. They are watching a Hindi movie.
6. He is watching a Hindi movie.
7. She is watching a Hindi movie.

Exercise 6.2

1. Maĩ skūl mẽ speech nahī̃ de rahā hū̃.
2. Ve restaurant mẽ khānā nahī̃ khā rahe haĩ.
3. Hum Hindi nahī̃ sikh rahe haĩ.
4. Āp daftar nahī̃ jā rahe haĩ.
5. Vah mandir mẽ bhajan nahī̃ gā rahā hai.
6. Vah ghar sāf nahī̃ kar rahī hai.
7. Tum so nahī̃ rahe ho.

१ मैं स्कूल में speech नहीं दे रहा हूँ ।
२ वे restaurant में खाना नहीं खा रहे हैं ।
३ हम हिन्दी नहीं सीख रहे हैं ।
४ आप दफ़्तर नहीं जा रहे हैं ।
५ वह मंदिर में भजन नहीं गा रहा है ।
६ वह घर साफ़ नहीं कर रही है ।
७ तुम सो नहीं रहे हो ।

Exercise 6.3

1. Āp nach rahe haĩ १ आप नाच रहे हैं ।
2. Vah so rahā hai. २ वह सो रहा है ।
3. Tum ro rahe ho. ३ तुम रो रहे हो ।
4. Hum music sun rahe haĩ. ४ हम music सुन रहे हैं ।
5. Ve hā̃s rahe haĩ. ५ वे हँस रहे हैं ।
6. Maĩ bartan dho rahī hū̃. ६ मैं बर्तन धो रही हूँ ।

Exercise 6.4

1. Kyā maĩ skūl mẽ speech de rahā hū̃?
2. Kyā ve restaurant mẽ khānā khā rahe haĩ?
3. Kyā hum Hindī sīkh rahe haĩ?
4. Kyā āp daftar jā rahe haĩ?
5. Kyā vah temple mẽ bhajan nahī̃ gā rahā hai?
6. Kyā vah ghar sāf nahī̃ kar rahī hai?

१ क्या मैं स्कूल में speech दे रहा हूँ ?
२ क्या वे restaurant में खाना खा रहे हैं ?
३ क्या हम हिन्दी सीख रहे हैं ?
४ क्या आप दफ़्तर जा रहे हैं ?
५ क्या वह temple में भजन नहीं गा रहा है ?
६ क्या वह घर साफ़ नहीं कर रही है ?

CHAPTER 7

Exercise 7.1

1. Vah ghar sāf <u>karegī</u>.
2. Hum Hindī <u>sīkhẽge</u>.
3. Āp daftar <u>jāẽge</u>.
4. Maĩ skūl mẽ speech <u>dū̃gā</u>.
5. Vah temple mẽ bhajan <u>gāegā</u>.
6. Ve restaurant mẽ khānā <u>khāẽge</u>.

१ वह घर साफ़ <u>करेगी</u> ।
२ हम हिन्दी <u>सीखेंगे</u> ।
३ आप दफ़्तर <u>जाएँगे</u> ।
४ मैं स्कूल में speech <u>दूँगा</u> ।
५ वह temple में भजन <u>गाएगा</u> ।
६ वे restaurant में खाना <u>खाएँगे</u> ।

Exercise 7.2

1. Viju uthegā.
2. Ve sikhẽge.
3. Sarah chāy piegī.
4. Hum ghar sāf karẽge.

१ Viju उठेगा ।
२ वे सीखेंगे ।
३ Sarah चाय पिएगी ।
४ हम घर साफ करेंगे ।

211

5 Bacche school jāẽge.   ५ बच्चे school जाएँगे ।
6 Maĩ ek patr likhū̃gā.   ६ मैं एक पत्र लिखूँगा ।

Exercise 7.3

1 Maĩ skūl mẽ speech nahī̃ dū̃gā.   १ मैं स्कूल में speech नहीं दूँगा ।
2 Ve restaurant mẽ khānā nahī̃ khāẽge.   २ वे restaurant में खाना नहीं खाएँगे ।
3 Hum Hindī nahī̃ sīkhẽge.   ३ हम हिन्दी नहीं सीखेंगे ।
4 Āp kal vahā̃ nahī̃ bolẽge.   ४ आप कल वहाँ नहीं बोलेंगे ।
5 Vah mujhse nahī̃ pūchegā.   ५ वह मुझसे नहीं पूछेगा ।
6 Vah javāb nahī̃ degī.   ६ वह जवाब नहीं देगी ।

Exercise 7.4

1. Kyā āp skūl mẽ speech dẽge?
2. Kyā ve seafood khāẽge?
3. Kyā ve Costa Rica ghūmẽge?
4. Kyā ve president se milẽge?
5. Kyā vah kal ceremony mẽ perform karegī?
6. Kyā vah ghar sāf karegī?

१ क्या आप स्कूल में speech देंगे ?
२ क्या वे seafood खाएँगे ?
३ क्या वे Costa Rica घूमेंगे ?
४ क्या वे president से मिलेंगे ?
५ क्या वह कल ceremony में perform करेगी ?
६ क्या वह घर साफ करेगी ?

Exercise 7.5

1 Kyā āp kal skūl mẽ speech nahī̃ dẽge?   १ क्या आप कल स्कूल में speech नहीं देंगे ?
2 Kyā ve nahī̃ bhūlẽge?   २ क्या वे नहीं भूलेंगें ?
3 Kyā hum ghar nahī̃ jāẽge?   ३ क्या हम घर नहीं जाएँगे ?
4 Kyā āp Italy mẽ nahī̃ rahẽge?   ४ क्या आप Italy में नहीं रहेंगे ?
5 Kyā maĩ acchā nahī̃ dikhū̃gā?   ५ क्या मैं अच्छा नहीं दिखूँगा ?

6 Kyā vah ghar ko sāf nahī̃ karegā?   ६ क्या वह घर को साफ नहीं करेगा ?

CHAPTER 8

Exercise 8.1

1 Maĩ Hindī movie dekhtā thā.   १ मैं हिन्दी movie देखता था ।
2 Maĩ Hindī movie dekhtī thī.   २ मैं हिन्दी movie देखती थी ।
3 Āp Hindī movie dekhte the.   ३ आप हिन्दी movie देखते थे ।
4 Hum Hindī movie dekhte the.   ४ हम हिन्दी movie देखते थे ।
5 Ve Hindī movie dekhte the.   ५ वे हिन्दी movie देखते थे ।
6 Vah Hindī movie dekhtā thā.   ६ वह हिन्दी movie देखता था ।
7 Vah Hindī movie dekhtī thī.   ७ वह हिन्दी movie देखती थी ।

1 I used to watch a Hindi movie. *(male)*
2 I used to watch a Hindi movie. *(female)*
3 You used to watch a Hindi movie.
4 We used to watch a Hindi movie.
5 They used to watch a Hindi movie.
6 He used to watch a Hindi movie.
7 She used to watch a Hindi movie.

Exercise 8.2

1 Maĩ skūl mẽ bhāshan <u>detā thā.</u>   १ मैं स्कूल में भाषण <u>देता था</u> ।
2 Vah ghar sāf <u>kartī thī.</u>   ६ वह घर साफ़ <u>करती थी</u> ।
3 Hum bhāshā <u>sīkhte the.</u>   ३ हम भाषा <u>सीखते थे</u> ।
4 Āp USPS mẽ kām <u>karte the.</u>   ४ आप USPS में काम <u>करते थे</u> ।
5 Vah temple mẽ bhajan <u>gātā thā.</u>   ५ वह temple में भजन <u>गाता था</u> ।
6 Ve restaurant mẽ Thai khānā <u>khāte the.</u> २ वे restaurant में Thai खाना <u>खाते थे</u> ।

Exercise 8.3

1. Maī skūl mẽ bhāshan nahī̃ detā thā.
2. Vah ghar sāf nahī̃ kartī thī.
3. Ham bhāshā nahī̃ sīkhte the.
4. Āp USPS mẽ kām nahī̃ karte the.
5. Vah temple mẽ bhajan nahī̃ gātā thā.
6. Ve restaurant mẽ khānaā nahī̃ khāte the.

१ मैं स्कूल में भाषण नहीं देता था ।
२ वह घर साफ़ नहीं करती थी ।
३ हम भाषा नहीं सीखते थे ।
४ आप USPS में काम नहीं करते थे ।
५ वह temple में भजन नहीं गाता था ।
६ वे restaurant में खाना नहीं खाते थे ।

Exercise 8.4

1. Kyā vah pitā thā?
2. Kyā vah cīzẽ bhūltī thī?
3. Kyā hum yahā̃ khelte the?
4. Kyā āp merī party mẽ āte the?
5. Kyā maī acchā dikhtā thā?
6. Kyā ve complain karte the?

१ क्या वह पीता था ?
२ क्या वह चीज़ें भूलती थी ?
३ क्या हम यहाँ खेलते थे ?
४ क्या आप मेरी party में आते थे ?
५ क्या मैं अच्छा दिखता था ?
६ क्या वे complain करते थे?

Exercise 8.5

Merā nām Alessia hai. Maī Chah baje uthtī <u>thī</u>. Phir, maī sādhe sāt baje tak taiyār <u>hotī</u> thī. Maī sādhe sāt baje se pā̃ch baje tak babysit kartī <u>thī</u>. Aur weekends pe navy drill pe <u>jātī</u> thī. Bād mẽ chār baje se pā̃ch baje tak, maī dinner <u>banātī</u> thī. Phir, maī ghar kā kām kartī <u>thī</u>.

मेरा नाम Alessia है । मैं छह बजे उठती <u>थी</u> । फिर, मैं साढ़े सात बजे तक तैयार <u>होती</u> थी । मैं साढ़े सात बजे से पाँच बजे तक babysit करती <u>थी</u> । और weekends पे navy drill पे <u>जाती</u> थी । बाद में चार बजे से पाँच बजे तक , मैं dinner <u>बनाती</u> थी । फिर , मैं घर का काम करती <u>थी</u> ।

CHAPTER 9

Exercise 9.1

1. Intransitive
2. Transitive
3. Transitive
4. Intransitive
5. Intransitive
6. Intransitive

Exercise 9.2

1	Maĩ bahut hāsā. *(male)*	१ मैं बहुत हँसा ।
2	Maĩ bahut hāsī. *(female)*	२ मैं बहुत हँसी ।
3	Āp bahut hāse.	३ आप बहुत हँसे ।
4	Hum bahut hāse.	४ हम बहुत हँसे ।
5	Ve bahut hāse.	५ वे बहुत हँसे ।
6	Vah bahut hāsā.	६ वह बहुत हँसा ।
7	Vah bahut hāsī.	७ वह बहुत हँसी ।

1. I laughed a lot. *(male)*
2. I laughed a lot. *(female)*
3. You laughed a lot.
4. We laughed a lot.
5. They laughed a lot.
6. He laughed a lot.
7. She laughed a lot.

Exercise 9.3

1	Maĩ skūl mẽ hāsā.	१ मैं स्कूल में हँसा ।
2	Ve restaurant mẽ roye.	२ वे restaurant में रोये ।

3 Hum French mẽ bole.   ३ हम French में बोले ।
4 Āp pool mẽ taire.   ४ आप pool में तैरे ।
5 Ve mandir mẽ mile.   ५ वे मंदिर में मिले ।
6 Vah ghar mẽ baithī.   ६ वह घर में बैठी ।

Exercise 9.4

1 Maĩ skūl mẽ nahī̃ hā̃sā.   १ मैं स्कूल में नहीं हँसा ।
2 Ve restaurant mẽ nahī̃ roye.   २ वे restaurant में नहीं रोये ।
3 Hum French mẽ nahī̃ bole.   ३ हम French में नहीं बोले ।
4 Āp pool mẽ nahī̃ taire.   ४ आप pool pool में नहीं तैरे ।
5 Ve mandir mẽ nahī̃ mile.   ५ वे मंदिर में नहीं मिले ।
6 Vah ghar mẽ nahī̃ baithī.   ६ वह घर में नहीं बैठी ।

Exercise 9.5

1 Ve kal rāt jangal mẽ <u>chale</u>.   १ वे कल रात जंगल में <u>चले</u> ।
2 Vah samay pe <u>uthā</u>.   २ वह समय पे <u>उठा</u> ।
3 Vah kal pool mẽ <u>tairī</u>.   ३ वह कल pool में <u>तैरी</u> ।
4 Hum bagīche mẽ kursiyõ pe baithī.   ४ हम बगीचे में कुर्सियों पे बैठी ।
5 Kyā āp subah merī bahan se <u>mile</u>?   ५ क्या आप सुबह मेरी बहन से <u>मिले</u> ?
6 Maĩ mere bete ke sāth Italian mẽ <u>bolā</u>.   ६ मैं मेरे बेटे के साथ Italian में <u>बोला</u> ।

Exercise 9.6

1 Ve jangal mẽ nahī̃ chale.   १ वे जंगल में नहीं चले ।
2 Kyā vah samay pe nahī̃ uthā ?   २ क्या वह समय पे नहीं उठा ?
3 Maĩ kal pool mẽ nahī̃ tairā.   ३ मैं कल pool में नहीं तैरा ।
4 Hum bagīche mẽ nahī̃ daude.   ४ हम बगीचे में नहीं दौड़े ।
5 Kyā vah party mẽ nachī ?   ५ क्या वह party में नाची ?
6 Kyā āp India mẽ rehe ?   ६ क्या आप India में रहे ?

1 They didn't walk in the forest.
2 Did he not get up on time?
3 I didn't swim in the pool yesterday.

4 We didn't run in the garden.
5 Did she dance at the party?
6 Did you live in India?

Exercise 9.7

1 Maīne chāy banāyī.
2 Maīne samose banāye.
3 Āpne rotiyā̃ banāyī̃.
4 Humne halwa banāyā.
5 Unhõne lassī banāyī.
6 Usne juice banāyā.
7 Usne ice-cream banāyī.

१ मैंने चाय बनाई ।
२ मैंने समोसे बनाये ।
३ आपने रोटियाँ बनायीं ।
४ हमने हलवा बनाया ।
५ उन्होंने लस्सी बनायी ।
६ उसने juice बनाया ।
७ उसने ice-cream बनायी ।

1 I made tea.
2 I made samosas.
3 You made rotis.
4 We made halwa.
5 They made lassi.
6 He made juice.
7 She made ice-cream.

Exercise 9.8

1 Maīne movie dekhī.
2 Usne "margherita" pizza nahī̃ khāyā.
3 Āpne camera nahī̃ kharīdā.
4 Humne Bollywood gīt sune.
5 Usne apne makān nahī̃ bechā
6 Unhõne spiritual bhajans gāye.
7 Maīne movie nahī̃ dekhī.
8 Āpne camera kharīdā.

१ मैंने movie देखी ।
२ उसने "margherita" pizza नहीं खाया ।
३ आपने camera नहीं ख़रीदा ।
४ हमने Bollywood गीत सुने ।
५ उसने अपने मकान नहीं बेचा ।
६ उन्होंने spiritual bhajans गाये ।
७ मैंने movie नहीं देखी ।
८ आपने camera ख़रीदा ।

Exercise 9.9

1 Kyā āpne movie dekhī?
2 Kyā usne "margherita" pizza khāyā?
3 Kyā humne Bollywood gīt sune?
4 Kyā unhone spiritual bhajans nahī̃ gāye?
5 Kyā āpne camera nahī̃ kharīdā?
6 Kyā usne makān nahī̃ bechā?

१ क्या आपने movie देखी ?
२ क्या उसने "margherita" pizza खाया ?
३ क्या हमने Bollywood गीत सुने ?
४ क्या उन्होंने spiritual bhajan नहीं गाए ?
५ क्या आपने camera नहीं ख़रीदा ?
६ क्या उसने मकान नहीं बेचा ?

CHAPTER 10

Exercise 10.1

1	Maī̃ Hindī mẽ likh saktā hū̃.	१ मैं हिन्दी में लिख सकता हूँ ।
2	Maī̃ Hindī mẽ likh saktī hū̃.	२ मैं हिन्दी में लिख सकती हूँ ।
3	Āp Hindī mẽ likh sakte haī̃.	३ आप हिन्दी में लिख सकते हैं ।
4	Hum Hindī mẽ likh sakte haī̃.	४ हम हिन्दी में लिख सकते हैं ।
5	Ve Hindī mẽ likh sakte haī̃.	५ वे हिन्दी में लिख सकते हैं ।
6	Vah Hindī mẽ likh saktā hai.	६ वह हिन्दी में लिख सकता है ।
7	Vah Hindī mẽ likh saktī hai.	७ वह हिन्दी में लिख सकती है ।

1 I can write in Hindi *(male)*
2 I can write in Hindi *(female)*
3 You can write in Hindi.
4 We can write in Hindi.
5 They can write in Hindi.
6 He can write in Hindi.
7 She can write in Hindi

Exercise 10.2

1 Maĩ professional cricket khel saktā hū̃.
2 Ve 10 ghante drive kar sakte haĩ.
3 Ham 10 bhāshāẽ bol aur likh sakte haĩ.
4 Āp non stop 12 ghante kām sakte haĩ.
5 Vah 5 dinõ mẽ ek software program develop kar saktā hai.
6 Vah 2 dinõ mẽ ek sweater bun saktī hai.

१ मैं professional cricket खेल सकता हूँ ।
२ वे दस घंटे drive कर सकते हैं ।
३ वह दस भाषाएँ बोल और लिख सकता है ।
४ आप non stop बारह घंटे काम सकते हैं ।
५ वह पाँच दिनों में एक software program develop कर सकता है ।
६ वह दो दिनों में एक sweater बुन सकती है ।

Exercise 10.3

1 Maĩ āpkī madad kar <u>saktā</u> hū̃.
2 Maĩ usko dekh nahī̃ <u>sakī</u>.
3 Usko roz din skūl jānā <u>chāhiye</u>.
4 Maĩ kitāb ko samay pe padh nahī̃ <u>sakā</u>.
5 Kyā āp kitāb ko padhnā <u>chāhte</u> haĩ?
6 Vah bahut acchā nach <u>saktī</u> hai.

१ मैं आपकी मदद कर <u>सकता</u> हूँ ।
२ मैं उसको देख नहीं <u>सकी</u> ।
३ उसको हर दिन स्कूल को जाना <u>चाहिए</u> ।
४ मैं किताब को समय पे नहीं पढ़ <u>सका</u> ।
५ क्या आप किताब को पढ़ना <u>चाहते</u> हैं ?
६ वह बहुत अच्छा नाच <u>सकती</u> है ।

CHAPTER 11

Exercise 11.1

1. Billī mez <u>pe</u> hai.
   The cat is on the table.

   १ बिल्ली मेज़ <u>पे</u> है ।

2. Vah <u>tumhāre liye</u> rotī banā rahī hai
   She is making bread for you.

   २ वह <u>तुम्हारे लिए</u> रोटी बना रही है ।

3. Tum <u>unke liye</u> gānā likh rahe ho.
   You are writing a song for them.

   ३ तुम <u>उनके लिए</u> गाना लिख रहे हो ।

4. <u>Usko</u> kitābẽ bahut pasand hai.
   She likes books very much.

   ४ <u>उसको</u> किताबें बहुत पसंद है ।

5. <u>Unko</u> bahut khushī hai.
   They are delighted.

   ५ <u>उनको</u> बहुत ख़ुशी है ।

Exercise 11.2

1. Maĩ palang pe baith rahā hũ.
2. Hum uske liye gīt gā rahe haĩ.
3. Usko bukhār hai. Usko dawāī chāhiye.
4. Tumko Hindī kahānīyā̃ bahut pasand hai.
5. Unko khānā banānā aatā hai.
6. Vah uskā intazār kar rahī hai.
7. Āpko ummīd hai.

१ मैं पलंग पे बैठ रहा हूँ ।
२ हम उसके लिए गीत गा रहे हैं ।
३ उसको बुखार है । उसको दवाई चाहिए ।
४ तुमको हिन्दी कहानियाँ बहुत पसंद है ।
५ उनको खाना बनाना आता है ।
६ वह उसका इंतज़ार कर रही है ।
७ आपको उम्मीद है ।

Exercise 11.3

1 Kyā maĩ palang pe baith rahā hū̃?
2 Kyā hum uske liye gīt gā rahe haĩ?
3 Kyā usko bukhār hai? Kyā Usko dawāī chāhiye?
4 Kyā tumko Hindī kahānīyā bahut pasand hai?
5 Kyā unko khānā banānā aatā hai?
6 Kyā vah uskā intazār kar rahī hai?
7 Kyā āpko ummīd hai?

१ क्या मैं पलंग पे बैठ रहा हूँ ?
२ क्या हम उसके लिए गीत गा रहे हैं ?
३ क्या उसको बुखार है ? क्या उसको दवाई चाहिए ?
४ क्या तुमको हिन्दी कहानियाँ बहुत पसंद है?
५ क्या उनको खाना बनाना आता है ?
६ क्या वह उसका इंतज़ार कर रही है ?
७ क्या आपको उम्मीद है ?

Exercise 11.4

1 Kyā āp kursī <u>pe</u> nahī̃ baithe?
   Didn't you sit on the chair?

2 Kyā ve uske <u>liye</u> kahānī nahī̃ likh rahe hai?
   Are they not writing a story for her?

3 Kyā <u>vah</u> abhī kām kar rahā hai?
   Is he working right now?

4 Kyā <u>āpko</u> dawāī nahī̃ chāhiye?
   Don't you need medicine?

5 Kya unko ummīd hai?
   Do they have hope?

6 Kyā <u>tumko</u> Address mālūm nahī̃ hai?
   Don't you know the Address?

7 Kya usko ice-cream <u>pasand</u> hai?
   Does he like ice-cream?

१ क्या आप कुर्सी <u>पे</u> नहीं बैठे ?
२ क्या वे उसके <u>लिए</u> कहानी नहीं लिख रहे है ?
३ क्या <u>वह</u> अभी काम कर रहा है ?
४ क्या <u>आपको</u> दवाई नहीं चाहिए ?
५ क्या उनको उम्मीद है ?
६ क्या <u>तुमको</u> हिन्दी मालूम नहीं है ?
७ क्या उसको ice-cream <u>पसंद</u> है ?

Exercise 11.5

1 Kapde ke nīche   १ कपड़े के नीचे ।
2 Kalam Ke nīche.   २ क़लम के नीचे ।
3 chāchā ke liye.   ३ chāchā के लिए ।
4 Ladke se.   ४ लड़के से ।

Exercise 11.6

1 Billī ped pe hai.   १ बिल्ली पेड़ पे है ।
2 Vah kuttõ se dartī hai.   २ वह कुत्तों से डरती है ।
3 Merā bhāī darvāze ke pīche hai.   ३ मेरा भाई दरवाज़े के पीछे है ।
4 Kyā āpkī kitāb mez ke pās hai?   ४ क्या आपकी किताब मेज़ के पास है ?

Exercise 11.7

1 Bahanẽ + ke liye = bahanõ ke liye   १ बहनें + के लिए = बहनों के लिए
2 Mezẽ + par = mezõ par   २ मेज़ें + पर = मेज़ों पर
3 Bhāshāẽ + ke bāre mẽ = bhāshāõ ke bāre mẽ   ३ भाषाएँ + के बारे में = भाषाओं के बारे में
4 Topīyā̃ + pe = topīyõ pe   ४ टोपियाँ + पे = टोपियों पे

Exercise 11.8

1 Vah gādī mẽ hai.
2 Chashme mezõ par hai.
3 Uskā dost kahāniyõ ke bāre mẽ bāt kar rahā hai.
4 Kyā āp movie ke bād soẽge?

१ वह गाड़ी में है ।
२ चश्मे मेज़ों पर है ।
३ उसका दोस्त कहानियों के बारे में बात कर रहा है ।
४ क्या आप movie के बाद सोएँगे ?

Exercise 11.9

1   Jūte, kursī *par* haĩ.
2   Chashmā, akhbār pe hai.
3   Akhbār, bistar pe hai.
4   Phul, mez pe hai.
5   Lamp, kitābõ ke ūpar / pe hai.
6   Bag, bistar ke pās haĩ.
7   Do pencils, kitāb pe haĩ.
8   Tīn tasvīrē̃, dīvār pe haĩ.
9   Chappalē̃, bistar ke nīche haĩ.
10 Ghaḍī, darāz ke ūpar hai.

१ जूते, कुर्सी पर हैं।
२ चश्मा अख़बार पे है।
३ अख़बार बिस्तर पे है।
४ फूल मेज़ पे है।
५ Lamp किताबों के ऊपर / पे है।
६ Bag बिस्तर के पास है।
७ दो pencils किताब पे हैं।
८ तीन तस्वीरें दीवार पे हैं।
९ चप्पलें बिस्तर के नीचे हैं।
१० घडी दराज़ के ऊपर है।

Exercise 11.10

1   Meri jeb <u>ke andar</u> āpkī chābiyā̃ haĩ.
    Your keys are in my pocket.

2   Uske ghar <u>ke bāhar</u> ek sundar bagīchā hai.
    There is a beautiful garden outside her/his house.

3   Vah <u>mere liye</u> acchī chāy banātī hai.
    She makes delicious tea for me.

4   Unke shehar <u>ke pās</u> ek lambī nadī hai.
    There is a big / long river near their town.

5   Maĩ Ady <u>ke sāth</u> Hindī kā homework karū̃gī.
    I will do my Hindi homework with Ady.

6   Tumharī gadī <u>ke ūpar</u> ek chhotī billī hai.

There is a small cat on top of your car .

१ मेरी जेब <u>के अंदर</u> आपकी चाबियाँ हैं ।
२ उसके घर <u>के बाहर</u> एक सुंदर बगीचा है ।
३ वह <u>मेरे लिए</u> अच्छी चाय बनाती है ।
४ उनके शहर <u>के पास</u> एक लंबी नदी है ।
५ मैं Ady <u>के साथ</u> हिन्दी का homework करूँगी ।
६ तुम्हारी गाड़ी <u>के ऊपर</u> एक छोटी बिल्ली है ।

Exercise 11.11

1 Maĩ + ko = mujh ko
2 Vah + mẽ = us mẽ
3 Tum + se = tum se
4 Hum + kī = humārī
5 Tum + ke bāre mẽ = tumhāre bāre mẽ
6 Tū + ke liye = Tere liye
7 Ve + ke bāhar = unke bāhar
8 Āp + ke sāth = āpke sāth

१ मैं + को = मुझ को
२ वह + में = उस में
३ तुम + से = तुम से
४ हम + की = हमारी
५ तुम + के बारे में = तुम्हारे बारे में
६ तू + के लिए = तेरे लिए
७ वे + के बाहर = उनके बाहर
८ आप + के साथ = आपके साथ

CHAPTER 12

Exercise 12.1

1 Āpkā patā kyā hai?
2 Kyā bāt hai?
3 Uski samasyā kyā hai?
4 Savāl kyā hai?
5 Javāb kyā hai?
6 Score kyā hai?

१ आपका पता क्या है ?
२ क्या बात है ? (this is not a yes/no question)
३ उसकी समस्या क्या है ?
४ सवाल क्या है ?
५ जवाब क्या है ?
६ Score क्या है ?

Exercise 12.2

1. Merā passport kahā̃ hai?
2. Āpki chābiyā̃ kahā̃ haĩ?
3. Uskā chasmā kahā̃ haĩ?
4. Ceremony kahā̃ hai?

१ मेरा passport कहाँ है ?
२ आपकी चाबियाँ कहाँ हैं ?
३ उसका चश्मा कहाँ है ?
४ Ceremony कहाँ है ?

Exercise 12.3

1. Unke parivār kaise haĩ?
2. Āpki Italy kī chuttīyā̃ kaisī thī?
3. Āpkā saptāhā̃t kaisā thā?
4. Yah klās kaisī hai?

१ उनके परिवार कैसे हैं ?
२ आपकी Italy की छुट्टियां कैसी थी ?
३ आपका सप्ताहाँत कैसा था ?
४ यह क्लास कैसी है ?

Exercise 12.4

1. Ve shehar kab ā rahe haĩ?
2. Āp Paris kab jāẽge?
3. Āp Hindī kā abhyās kab karte haĩ?
4. Āp kab paidā hue?

१ वे शहर कब आ रहे हैं ?
२ आप Paris कब जाएँगे ?
३ आप हिन्दी का अभ्यास कब करते हैं ?
४ आप कब पैदा हुए ?

Exercise 12.5

1. Donald Trump kaun hai?
2. Chāy kaun banā saktā hai?
3. Kal āpki party mē kaun āyā?
4. Javāb kaun jāntā hai?

१ Donald Trump कौन है ?
२ चाय कौन बना सकता है ?
३ कल आपकी party में कौन आया ?
४ जवाब कौन जानता है ?

Exercise 12.6

1. Kaun sī klās ?
2. Kaun sī relgāḍī?
3. Kaun sā jānvar?

    4   Mujko kaun se jūte pahnne chāhiye?
    5   Mujhko kaun sī davāī kharīdnī chāhiye?
    6   Āpko kaun sā khel/khelkūd pasand hai?
    7   Āp kaun sī bhāshā bolte haĩ?

१ कौन सी क्लास ?
२ कौन सी रेलगाड़ी ?
३ कौन सा जानवर ?
४ मुझको कौन से जूते पहनने चाहिए ?
५ मुझको कौन सी दवाई खरीदनी चाहिए ?
६ आपको कौन सा खेल / खेलकूद पसंद है ?
७ आप कौन सी भाषा बोलते हैं ?

Exercise 12.7

1 Ākāsh nīlā kyõ hai?
2 Āp Hindī kyõ sīkh rahe haĩ?
3 Vah javāb kyõ nahī̃ de saktī hai?
4 Mujhko paiṭ dard kyõ ho rahā hai?
5 Ve humāre ghar kyõ nahī̃ ā rahe haĩ?

१ आकाश नीला क्यों है ?
२ आप हिन्दी क्यों सीख रहे हैं ?
३ वह जवाब क्यों नहीं दे सकती है ?
४ मुझको पेट दर्द क्यों हो रहा है ?
५ वे हमारे घर क्यों नहीं आ रहे हैं ?

CHAPTER 13

Exercise 13.1

<u>Purānā</u>	purānī kursī - purāne jūte - purānā ghar - purānī kitābẽ
<u>Sundar</u>	sundar kursī - sundar jūte - sundar ghar - sundar kitābẽ
<u>Ākhirī</u>	ākhirī kursī - ākhirī jūte - ākhirī ghar - ākhirī kitābẽ
<u>Gandā</u>	gandī kursī - gande jūte - gandā ghar - gandī kitābẽ

<u>पुराना</u>	पुरानी कुर्सी - पुराने जूते - पुराना घर - पुरानी किताबें
<u>सुंदर</u>	सुंदर कुर्सी - सुंदर जूते - सुंदर घर - सुंदर किताबें
<u>आखिरी</u>	आखिरी कुर्सी - आखिरी जूते - आखिरी घर - आखिरी किताबें
<u>गंदा</u>	गन्दी कुर्सी - गंदे जूते - गंदा घर - गन्दी किताबें

Exercise 13.2

1 Chhote ladke kā bhāī.
2 Chhote ladkõ kā bhāī.
3 Chhotī ladkī kā bhāī.
4 Chhotī ladkiõ kā bhāī.

१ छोटे लड़के का भाई ।
२ छोटे लड़कों का भाई ।
३ छोटी लड़की का भाई ।
४ छोटी लड़कियों का भाई ।

Exercise 13.3

1 Ve gādī ke āge chal rahe the.
2 Vah ek safed gādī chalā rahī thī.
3 Vah pīlā phūl kharīd rahā hai.
4 Ham nīli nadī mẽ tair rahe haĩ.
5 Sarah garam curry nahī̃ khā rahi hai.
6 Kyā vah India se naī sārī kharīd rahī hai?

१ वे गाड़ी के आगे चल रहे थे ।
२ वह एक सफ़ेद गाड़ी चला रही थी ।
३ वह पीला फूल खरीद रहा है ।
४ हम नीली नदी में तैर रहे हैं ।
५ Sarah गरम curry नहीं खा रही है ।
६ क्या वह India से नई साड़ी खरीद रही है ?

CHAPTER 14

Exercise 14.1

1 Usne āsānī se game jītā.
2 Unhone jaldī se 911 call kiyā.
3 Maĩ zor se hãsā.
4 Āpne dhyān se traffic mẽ gādī calāyī.

१ उसने आसानी से game जीता ।
२ उन्होंने जल्दी से 911 call किया ।
३ मैं ज़ोर से हँसा ।
४ आपने ध्यान से traffic में गाड़ी चलायी ।

1 She won the game easily..
2 They called 911 quickly.
3 I laughed loudly.
4 You drove carefully in traffic.

Exercise 14.2

1 Maĩ skūl mẽ zor se hãsā.
2 Ve restaurant mẽ dhīre se bole.
3 Hum French fluently bole.
4 Āp pool mẽ ālas se taire.
5 Ve mandir mẽ gupt tarike se mile.
6 Vah ghar mẽ khushī-khushī baithī.

१ मैं स्कूल में ज़ोर से हँसा ।
२ वे restaurant में धीरे से बोले ।
३ हम French fluently बोले ।
४ आप pool में आलस से तैरे ।
५ वे मंदिर में गुप्त tarike से मिले ।
६ वह घर में ख़ुशी-ख़ुशी बैठी ।

Exercise 14.3

1 Kyā āp skūl mẽ zor se hãse?
2 Ve restaurant mẽ dhīre se nahī̃ bole.
3 Kyā vah French fluently bolī?
4 Kyā āp pool mẽ ālas se taire?
5 Kyā ve mandir mẽ gupt tarike se nahī̃ mile?
6 Vah ghar mẽ khushī-khushī nahī̃ baithī.

१ क्या आप स्कूल में ज़ोर से हँसे ?
२ वे restaurant में धीरे से नहीं बोले ।
३ क्या वह French fluently बोली ?
४ क्या आप pool में आलस से तैरे ?
५ क्या वे मंदिर में गुप्त तरीके से नहीं मिले ?
६ वह घर में ख़ुशी-ख़ुशी नहीं बैठी ।

Exercise 14.4

1 Usne hal hī mẽ ek kitāb likhī.
2 Maĩ mere bhāī ko bād mẽ dekhū̃gī.

228

3 Āp abhī kyā kar rahe haĩ?
4 Kyā ve abhī tak khā rahe haĩ?
5 Hum pehle movie nahī̃ dekh rahe the.
6 Vah jaldī hī uskī nayī naukrī shurū karegī.

१ उसने हाल ही में एक किताब लिखी ।
२ मैं मेरे भाई को बाद में देखूँगी ।
३ आप अभी क्या कर रहे हैं ?
४ क्या वे अभी तक खा रहे हैं ?
५ हम पहले movie नहीं देख रहे थे ।
६ वह जल्दी ही उसकी नयी नौकरी शुरू करेगी ।

Exercise 14.5

1 Yah gānā <u>vāstav</u> mẽ accha hai.
2 Āp uskī kitāb <u>har jagah</u> kharīd sakte haĩ.
3 Hum uske bāre mẽ <u>thodā</u> pareshān hote haĩ.
4 Vah is sāl <u>kahī̃ bhī</u> nahī̃ jā rahī hai.
5 Ve <u>bahut</u> khush haĩ kyõ ki unhõne ek nayā ghar kharīdā.
6 Maĩ is saptāh <u>kahī̃ nahī̃</u> jānā chāhtī hū̃.

१ यह गाना <u>वास्तव</u> में अच्छा है ।
२ आप उसकी किताब <u>हर जगह</u> खरीद सकते हैं ।
३ हम उसके बारे में <u>थोड़ा</u> परेशान होते हैं ।
४ वह इस साल <u>कहीं भी</u> नहीं जा रही है ।
५ वे <u>बहुत</u> ख़ुश हैं क्यों कि उन्होंने एक नया घर ख़रीदा ।
६ मैं इस सप्ताह <u>कहीं नहीं</u> जाना चाहती हूँ ।

1 This song is lovely.
2 You can buy his book everywhere.
3 We are a little worried about him.
4 She is not going anywhere this year.
5 They are delighted because they bought a new house.
6 There is nowhere I want to go this week

What's next?

Let us congratulate Pingu on successfully completing this Hindi workbook. She is excited as ever and can't wait to practice Hindi with other students. She wants to watch Bollywood movies and sing songs, she wants to travel to India and talk to people on Indian streets. Her first mission is accomplished as she has all the tools and the confidence to speak in Hindi.

But wait, Pingu's and your journey to learning Hindi is not yet over. Continue this exciting journey with HindiUniversity and connect with other zealous budding Hindi speakers from around the world. Click on the links below and embark today!

Watch HindiUniversity Videos and join free Sunday classes	https://tiny.cc/hindiuniversity
Subscribe to HindiUniversity	https://www.youtube.com/c/hindiuniversity
Join our mailing list	http://tinyurl.com/hindiuniv
Practice Hindi with Duolingo	https://www.duolingo.com/course/hi/en/Learn-Hindi
Translate from your language to Hindi and vice-versa	https://translate.google.com/
Write in the Devanagari	https://www.google.com/inputtools/try/
Become friends with Ashu	https://www.facebook.com/hindi101
Support HindiUniversity	https://www.paypal.me/hindiuniversity
Test your Hindi skills	Hindi Exam - Part 1
	Hindi Exam - Part 2
Learn Devanagari	https://www.learning-hindi.com/
Contact HindiUniversity	ashutosa.2009@gmail.com

If you notice any unintended mistakes, please report them at ashutosa.2009@gmail.com and help us improve.

To the reader

This book is a result of tireless and selfless efforts by several HindiUniversity students over many months. Their enthusiasm is contagious, and their energy is uplifting. It has been a privilege to witness this book's evolution, which started with a general concept and morphed quickly into a workbook, developed with input from students from around the world who are actively learning Hindi. All images at the beginning of each chapter are handmade. All exercises, essays, edits, romanagari texts, Devanagari texts, tables, cover page, and so many minute details of this book are a testament to the hard work put in by the HindiUniversity students. I am forever indebted to each one of them. I want to specifically acknowledge the extraordinary effort put in by Elham Golfam (Iran) and Cecilia Rodica Moanṭă (Spain) for giving life and meaning to the book.

The best part of my week is standing in front of my students via HindiUniversity and interacting with them during our live classes. I have not met most of the students in real life and perhaps may never meet them in person, but we have developed a deep connection over these years and have become one family. To me, these rewarding experiences are invaluable.

To be clear, I am neither a linguist nor do I hold any academic degree in Hindi. However, in all these years of teaching, I have learned that language learning can be simplified; students should be encouraged to make mistakes, learn from them, and continue to practice until they master the skill. I thoroughly enjoyed writing this book, and I hope you see the hard work put in by the HindiUniversity students. If there are any unintended mistakes, I hope you can still focus on the bigger picture of language learning. I hope to see you in a HindiUniversity live class one day.

Hello! My name is Liz, and I live in Denver, Colorado USA. I am so very grateful that Ashu ji has created the HindiUniversity and shared his knowledge with us. He is a friendly teacher with the ability to explain things well. I have enjoyed learning Hindi from him and enjoyed the atmosphere that he continues to develop. I have also enjoyed the friendships in this class.

I am Chelsea from the United States. I have been learning Hindi since about 2009. It is a beautiful, exciting, and challenging language! I really enjoy the HindiUniversity format because it gives the students a solid understanding of grammar and speaking practice.

My name is Agnes. I study Hindi. I love India and its culture. Ashu ji has given us the opportunity to learn and to make new friends at the same time! Thanks Ashu ji!

My journey to learning Hindi started around 3 years ago. Learning Hindi can sometimes feel daunting, as there isn't an active local Hindi-learning community where I live. Thanks to Ashu ji and his HindiUniversity, now I have a fantastic community of Hindi learners to help me through the hurdles. Ashu ji keeps Hindi learning what it should be fun! His brilliant understanding of all the grammar nuances, systematic and logical approach, and variety of materials make Hindi learning feel much easier and enjoyable. His incredible patience, dedication, and enthusiasm are the reason I feel inspired to keep learning more about this beautiful language. Thank you Ashu ji, for creating this wonderful community for us. Marcel from Slovakia.

Thank you Ashu ji for everything, especially for making me not give up on Hindi when I felt I was too lost with the language. Anne Laurence from France.

I am very thankful to Ashu ji for helping me learn the Hindi language which has helped much in my job! Rita Moore from the US.

Hello Ashu ji, thank you for all the lessons all these years. Greetings, Teresa from the Netherlands.

Hi, I am Jirka from Czechia and I am learning Hindi! The reason is simple, I would like to go to India, and be able to speak with the locals in their own language. When I started learning, it all seemed simple - I would just learn how to write/read and then some essential phrases and essential vocabulary. But then? Then I got stuck, I did not know how to proceed with my learning, I needed someone to explain many things to me and to answer all of my questions. I have tried many approaches, but I was still missing some structure, system and guidance. Then I found the HindiUniversity, which is a community of people learning Hindi language led by Ashutosh from India.

Hi. My name is Alessia and I am from Italy. I like Hindi films and songs, so I'd like to learn the language just to be able to understand them a little better. In this lovely community, I found many people who share my interests and Ashu ji's classes are just excellent help.

Hello Ashu ji, Greetings from Myanmar. First I would like to say thank you so much for teaching and supporting us in the Hindi Language. I got confident in learning Hindi after joining your online class. We appreciate that you are the best and patient guru in teaching the Hindi language. Sincerely, Than!

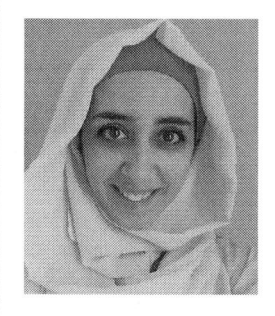

I am Tasnim from jordan, Middle East, I started my Hindi learning since 2007 but I never felt as confident to speak Hindi as I felt after less than 10 lessons with teacher Ashu ji, I am pleased to be a student with him, he encourages me and supports me to find out the answer and provides all great explanations I need. classes are great thank you teacher Ashu ji

"I saw two of Ashu ji's programs on youtube about one year ago and realized immediately that it was exactly what I wanted and needed for being able to improve my basic Hindi. When I wrote a message to him thanking him for his excellent teaching , he answered me and explained that there were about 500 lessons more! Heaven opened for me!Yes , I was in seventh heaven! He is a great teacher , he is there for his students, he knows how to teach! I have visited India twice every year for many years and I do try,want and love to get in contact with Indian people by using their beautiful language. I am crazy about India and Hindi. Why? Many people ask me that question, but there is no clear answer. I am longing to go back there all the time. Thanks Ashu ji for your help and inspiration!

Hi, my name is Navaneeth. I am currently living in California, United States. I started studying Hindi in an organization for a few years. Unfortunately, the center closed which resulted in a temporary halt in my hindi studies until I came to know about hindiuniversity. I started attending Ashu ji's classes which helped me to continue my hindi studies. I am really thankful to Ashu ji for all his efforts in teaching us hindi. He encourages me to share my opinions. His amazing understanding of all the grammar nuances, systematic and logical approach makes hindi learning feel much more enjoyable. Thank you Ashu ji for encouraging me to keep on learning hindi!

The HindiUniversity has become my only resource in my Hindi learning journey since I discovered it a few months ago. Before this, I always struggled with navigating through the numerous tenses and grammar rules. (Aur koi maza nahi aa raha tha) The HindiUniversity has a comprehensive database of videos which are strategically organised in one space. (Mujhe aisa laga ki ab Hindi seekhne mein koi rukaavat nahi hai.) It's as simple as choosing a topic and learning from the fun, easy-to-follow videos. (Zindagi aur aasaan nahi ho sakti) In addition to this, a weekly online class is held. This has become my most enjoyable Hindi learning experience. The classes are interactive and topics are expertly covered so it's easy to understand even with no prior knowledge of the topic. Time is allocated during the classes specifically to practice speaking in Hindi with fellow students. I find that my fluency in speaking has improved quite a lot in a short space of time. Main Ashu ji ka bahut abhaari hun. Sangeeta - Trinidad and Tobago

My name is Madhuvrata Das, I'm from Poland but have been living in India for 3 years as a brahmacari monk in ISKCON temple. I live in India because I understand the tremendous value of ancient Indian culture and knowledge, and want to make an attempt, to remind Indians about the importance of their own heritage, which they tend to undervalue. This is the main reason why I've been learning Hindi. I have been learning Hindi for 1 year. Beginnings are relatively easy but at a certain point I became stuck and although surrounded by natives couldn't make much progress. Everyone says - "Just try to speak somehow and in that way you'll learn." But it doesn't work with me. Then Ashutosh ji came into picture and he gave me impetus and systematized my learning. I'm very grateful and hope that one day we will meet, while you will be visiting your relatives in India, Ashutosh ji. Thank you, Hare Krishna

I am Dhanraj Singh from Trinidad and Tobago, West Indies, I started learning Hindi when I was 10 years old. But somehow I did not manage to study it further. Now that I am introduced to Ashu ji and his online HindiUniversity I am motivated to study Hindi further. Hindi language is an integral part of the cultural tapestry of Indian Caribbean people.

Hello, My name is Jamil. I am from Azerbaijan. I had my first impressions about India in childhood. My family and I used to watch old Indian movies. The colorful culture of India became so interesting for me. Years passed and now I am working in the tourism industry, so it gives me a chance to meet different people from all over the world. One of the biggest tourist groups to Azerbaijan is from India. Since I have started to communicate with them, I have decided to learn Hindi. It made me so happy when I found the "HindiUniversity'' channel on Youtube, because of this channel and Mr. Ashutosh I can communicate with people in this language just in a short time. A new world and really ancient culture is in front of me now!

Namaste! My name is Aditya and I'm from Norway. Being an adoptee, I have a strong connection to India, since it's my country of birth. For many years I have wanted to learn Hindi and I was so pleased when I discovered "HindiUniversity" on Youtube. Online classes which are so easy accessible and fun.
Thank you so much Ashu ji, for your lectures and inspiration. I am forever grateful! Not only for teaching me the most beautiful language there is, but also helping me connect deeper with my roots.

Namaste, My name is Hanady, I am from Egypt. Ashu ji, I learned a lot in your class because you took the extra time to explain things clearly. You gave us the extra help we needed. Thank you for giving us your time. Thank you for creating such a great environment to learn and where we were encouraged to express our own thoughts and opinions. Attending your classes was always like taking a deep dive into an ocean full of knowledge and wisdom. You are the best teacher ever! Thank you! Pranaam, Jai Hind

Thanks to Ashu-ji, my Hindi has improved dramatically. I wanted to learn Hindi to speak with my grandparents better and also my family in India. Now, thanks to his lessons, I am able to communicate with them effectively and have deeper conversations. While I have been exposed to Hindi since I was young, it was not until I discovered Ashu-ji's lectures and started attending his class that I truly understood the language. Ashu-ji, you are truly a wonderful teacher and I am thankful for all the work you do to spread our Hindi language. Vedant from New York

It was a chance sighting on Google that brought me to HindiUniversity. I needed a challenge when I retired and decided to intensify my learning of Hindi. I travel a lot to India. Its culture has been a long-held fascination for me. I wanted to experience parts of India from a different perspective. Connecting with HindiUniversity has supported me towards attaining my goal of fluency. Ashu's live online classes are easy to follow but cover topics in depth. They are also available as recordings to view again at any time. This is a bonus for me as I travel a lot and they help me maintain the momentum of my studies. I recommend Ashu for his knowledge and ability to explain difficult concepts. He is also generous of his time, good humoured and supportive of his students.

Namaste. Mera nam Maud hai. (Maddy klass ke liye). Je voulais apprendre l'hindi et je ne sais plus comment je suis tombée sur hindu university et depuis fin septembre 2018 je suis les cours avec Ashu ji. Mujhe hindi seekhna bahut pasand hai. Hamare adhyapack Ashu ji est très patient, très calme. Vah har haphte apana samay hamaare lie samarpit karta hai et nous encourage à ne pas abandonner. Bahut dhanyavaad Ashu ji. Shabash. Aap iske laayak hai. Maddy. De la Guadeloupe.

Namaste!! I am Itzel from México. I have been studying Hindi for 4 years by myself, however the videos of the HindiUniversity channel have been an important learning tool for me. I have the opportunity to attend his classes and I can see that Ashu ji has great passion and patience in teaching.

Thanks for everything Ashu ji !!!.

I'm Flavio, originally from Brazil, but living in Irving, TX. Hindi is a beautiful language, and I really appreciate the wonderful job Ashu ji does, making it accessible to people all over the world. And the way he teaches makes anyone learn the language easily. Please keep up the good job!

Namaskar! mera naam Nawras hai. Main arab hoon. Mujhe bharat ke philosophy aur culture bahut pasand hai. Kyunki mujhe Sanskrit sikhana hai, isliye maine hindi sikhna shuro kiya. main jaanti hoon rashta bahuat lamba hai, par hume kahi na kahi se shruwat karni hi hoti hain. Pahle maine kud se hindi sikana shru kiya. phir main kuch bahut acche bharatey dosto se mili. unhone mere bahut madad ki. phir mujhe ek din Ashu ji ke channel mila. main unke classes mein shamil ho gyi. Ashu ji bahut dhairy ke saath padhate hain. We nisvaarth se kaam karte hain. Ashutosh ji Bina kisi apeksha ke hume sikhate hain. unke kaam ke liye dhanywaad kaafi nahi hai. Bhagwan Ashutosh ji ko hamesha khush rakhe.

I began my Hindi learning journey in 2007 here in Berkeley, CA USA at the local university. It was intense and stressful. Then…life. In 2020, I returned to Hindi. While googling, I came across Ashu-ji and Hindi University. What a gift! Ashu-ji makes Hindi really fun and his teachings have motivated me to practice everyday. He is kind, patient, warm and generous as a teacher. In the videos, he is clear and concise. He also gives helpful formulas for sentence construction. In the live classes Ashu-ji models that it's OK to make mistakes, he encourages and praises our efforts and he waits patiently as we finish our attempts. Finally, at this time when travel is not possible, I'm getting to know people from all over the world. Thank you Ashu-ji for creating a beautiful community. Peace, Kelly

My name is Jennifer Nash. I am a professor at Duke University. I met Ashu-ji many years ago when we both lived in Washington DC, and I started taking weekly Hindi lessons with him. I've loved watching HU grow, and I have loved seeing Ashu's love of Hindi and compassionate teaching touch people across the globe.

I was born in India but have been living in Taiwan for over 30 years now. I teach Hindi conversation here to Taiwanese. While teaching, I started to face some challenges because students would ask questions related to Hindi grammar, which I did not know much about. My search brought me to Hindi University and I was very thrilled to find such a treasure trove of useful resources. I was so impressed that I even encouraged my own children to join the class so that they can learn Hindi as well. Finally, I would encourage Hindi Learners to take the testing system offered by Hindi University, which provides a certificate if a student passes. Happy Learning! Priya from Taiwan

My name is Jaweher . I'm a tunisian student. I got interested in the indian culture at a very young age due to Bollywood movies. But my country isn't unfortunately one of those who are so familiar with india related stuff, so i had no way of learning hindi here. I had to learn on my own so I tried lots of ways. And one of the best things that happened to me during the learning process was HU. Ashu ji helped me a lot and his lessons are ultimately the best. I'm really glad i found him.

I am grateful that Ashu ji, our very best and patient guru, has brought us all together from all over the world to share this wonderful experience! Learning Hindi and learning about India and its culture has enriched my life! Thank you! Lia, Romania & Spain.

Years ago I learned several Hindi words and sentences from a friend but I didn't continue. Some years later, I decided to start learning Hindi again. I used Hindi language learning sites, applications, etc., but yet many things weren't clear to me. I once watched a Hindi learning video. The video started like this: "Namaste everyone. Welcome to HindiUniversity. My name is Ashutosh...". It seemed amazing to me, so I decided to participate in HindiUniversity class and I did. It was wonderful. Classmates from different countries and a great teacher who is extremely patient and kind. He gives time to teach his students honestly. Now, he really is one of my best teachers and Hindi is so much clearer to me.

Simply but deeply thank you Guru ji. Tara from Iran

Printed in Great Britain
by Amazon